T0323712

# Cambridge Elements ☰

**Elements in Bioethics and Neuroethics**
edited by
Thomasine Kushner
*California Pacific Medical Center, San Francisco*

# THE ETHICS OF CONSCIOUSNESS

Walter Glannon
*University of Calgary*

CAMBRIDGE
UNIVERSITY PRESS

# CAMBRIDGE
## UNIVERSITY PRESS

University Printing House, Cambridge CB2 8BS, United Kingdom

One Liberty Plaza, 20th Floor, New York, NY 10006, USA

477 Williamstown Road, Port Melbourne, VIC 3207, Australia

314–321, 3rd Floor, Plot 3, Splendor Forum, Jasola District Centre, New Delhi – 110025, India

103 Penang Road, #05–06/07, Visioncrest Commercial, Singapore 238467

Cambridge University Press is part of the University of Cambridge.

It furthers the University's mission by disseminating knowledge in the pursuit of education, learning, and research at the highest international levels of excellence.

www.cambridge.org
Information on this title: www.cambridge.org/9781009078047
DOI: 10.1017/9781009086660

First published 2022

*A catalogue record for this publication is available from the British Library.*

ISBN 978-1-009-07804-7 Paperback
ISSN 2752-3934 (online)
ISSN 2752-3926 (print)

# The Ethics of Consciousness

Elements in Bioethics and Neuroethics

DOI: 10.1017/9781009086660
First published online: June 2022

Walter Glannon
*University of Calgary*

**Author for correspondence:** Walter Glannon, wglannon@ucalgary.ca

**Abstract:** This Element examines the main ethical aspects of consciousness. It argues that consciousness is not intrinsically valuable but has value or disvalue for individuals depending on its phenomenology (what it is like to be aware) and content (what one is aware of). These two components of awareness shape normative judgments about how ordered, disordered, altered, restored, diminished, and suppressed conscious states can benefit or harm individuals. They also influence moral judgments about whether intentionally causing these states is permissible or impermissible and how these states can affect behavior. After describing its neurobiological basis, the Element discusses ethical and legal issues in six categories of consciousness: phenomenal and access consciousness, intraoperative awareness, prolonged disorders of consciousness, dissociative disorders, the role of consciousness in determining death, and altering and suppressing awareness near the end of life.

**Keywords:** arousal, awareness, benefit, brain death, consciousness, continuous deep sedation dissociative disorders, harm, prolonged disorders of consciousness, terminal anesthesia

ISBNs: 9781009078047 (PB), 9781009086660 (OC)
ISSNs: 2752-3934 (online), 2752-3926 (print)

# Contents

# 1 Introduction

Consciousness arguably has been discussed more than any other topic in philosophy and neuroscience. Philosophers have focused primarily on what David Chalmers describes as the "hard problem" of consciousness: How and why does subjective experience arise from the physical brain?[1] How does gray and white matter in distributed neural networks generate the feeling of what it is like to perceive or be something?[2] Chalmers distinguishes this from what he describes as the "easy problem" of consciousness. This consists in explaining how information is processed in the brain by sensory systems and how this processing influences thought and behavior. Regarding the hard problem, Chalmers states: "Even when we have explained the performance of all the cognitive and behavioral functions in the vicinity of experience – perceptual discrimination, categorization, internal access, verbal report – there may still remain a further unanswered question: Why is the performance of these functions accompanied by experience?"[3] Whether the hard problem of consciousness will be solved remains an open question.

Neuroscientists have focused on the neural substrate of consciousness and how it enables arousal, or wakefulness, and awareness of self and the surrounding environment. The neural correlates of consciousness (NCCs) "are the minimum neural mechanisms jointly sufficient for any one specific conscious experience."[4] Christof Koch and coauthors distinguish:

> Full NCC (the neural substrate supporting experience in general, irrespective of its specific content), content-specific NCC (the neural substrate supporting a particular content of experience – for example, faces, whether they seem dreamt or imagined), and background conditions (factors that enable consciousness, but do not contribute directly to the content of the experience – for example, arousal systems that ensure adequate excitability of the NCC).[5]

Clinical neuroscientists have investigated how anesthesia, brain injury, and neurodevelopmental and neurodegenerative diseases suppress or disable this neural substrate and diminish or permanently eliminate the capacity for consciousness. They have also investigated how psychopharmacological and other interventions might restore this capacity.

There is a normative ethical dimension to consciousness. This involves questions about the permissibility or impermissibility of actions that alter, suppress, or restore awareness. It also involves questions about how these actions and other events affecting the brain's capacity to generate and sustain awareness can benefit or harm people, as well as judgments about actions performed in altered conscious states. Although they have different historical meanings, "ethical" and "moral" are often used interchangeably, and I follow this practice here. "Benefit" refers to events that realize or satisfy a person's interests. "Harm" refers to events that thwart or defeat these interests.[6] A person benefits from an action when it makes her better off and is harmed when it makes her worse off. Interests are based on conscious mental states such as desires and beliefs about events that can affect persons, their bodies, and their lives. They are components of a person's well-being, measured roughly in terms of one's level of functional independence and quality of life.[7] If interests extend to the end of one's biological life, then individuals could benefit from or be harmed by events after they have permanently lost the capacity for consciousness.[8] This may include events occurring after death.[8] There can be both experiential and nonexperiential benefit and harm, depending on the connection between a person's interests and the presence or absence of consciousness.

The phenomenal aspect of consciousness (what it is like to be aware) and its content (what one is aware of) are not determined solely by its underlying neural substrate. They are also shaped by the body and the natural and social environment in which one lives and acts.[9] This is what makes consciousness ethically significant. As Chris Frith points out, "all the contents of consciousness are the outcome of a social endeavor."[10] Emphasizing this same idea, Adam Zeman states that the function of consciousness is to "free the organism from control by its immediate environment" by enabling flexible and adaptive behavior within it. He adds that, as conscious subjects, we "are in and of the world from the start."[11] The brain is "an enabler – an instrument that brings us into contact with the world."[12] The ethical issues associated with consciousness involve not just what is inside the head but also what extends beyond it.

For many, the capacity for consciousness is an essential property of being a person. But consciousness as such does not have intrinsic value. By themselves, arousal and awareness have no moral significance. What makes them significant is that they enable us to think, feel, and act. The capacity for consciousness has value when it enables us to adapt to the environment and engage in meaningful mental and physical activities at specific times and over time. The loss of this capacity in irreversible unconsciousness has disvalue because it permanently deprives us of this ability. Awareness can also have disvalue, as in the experience of acute and chronic pain, depression, and anxiety. "It is the contents of consciousness that make it either good or bad. Experiences of love, pleasure, beauty, etc. are good, while experiences of pain, suffering, isolation, loneliness etc. are bad."[13] The phenomenal aspect of pain and other forms of experience can also make them good or bad. Awareness can be the source of both benefit and harm by generating and realizing or thwarting our interests and action plans in the sorts of experience we want to have or avoid.

Depending on its phenomenology and content and how they affect people, consciousness can have value or disvalue for them.[14]

Different authors have discussed some of the ethical issues surrounding consciousness. These include how prolonged disorders of consciousness (DOCs) affect individual well-being,[15] whether minimal awareness is better than none,[16] and whether continuing or discontinuing life-sustaining treatment for patients with these disorders can be morally justified.[17] There are in fact both ethical and legal implications to these questions. In many cases, courts adjudicate conflicts between parties making decisions about them. In addition, there is the question of whether individuals with dissociative disorders can be morally and criminally responsible for their actions.[18] There is also the question of whether inducing unconsciousness at the end of life with sedation or anesthesia is permissible.[19] The normative dimensions of full, impaired, or altered consciousness, and unconsciousness, involve these and other issues. This Element is an integrated analysis and discussion of them.

Discussion of the ethics of consciousness must be framed by the neurobiology of consciousness. Although the neural correlates of awareness cannot explain moral judgments about benefit, harm, or responsibility, they are necessary to explain the neural source behind these normative categories and thus necessary to inform these judgments. In Section 2, I describe different neurobiological models of consciousness and explain how disruption of connectivity in neural networks can temporarily or permanently impair or suppress arousal and awareness. In Section 3, I examine the differences between phenomenal and access consciousness. In Section 4, I discuss how actions and other events occurring at both conscious and unconscious levels during general anesthesia can affect patients' experience and behavior intraoperatively and postoperatively. This is followed by Section 5 with an analysis of prolonged DOCs and interventions that could restore awareness and cognitive and motor functions for patients with these disorders. It includes discussion of the challenges in conducting research with these interventions. I compare the minimally conscious state (MCS) and the vegetative state (VS) and consider reasons why each of these states may be better or worse than the other for patients who are in them. I also consider technology that would allow nonresponsive patients to communicate wishes about life-sustaining care.

In Section 6, I examine dissociative disorders, how they can impair agency, and whether individuals exhibiting seemingly automatic behavior could be responsible for their actions. I then discuss how the capacity for consciousness figures in debates about determining death in Section 7. Regarding deceased organ donation, I consider whether patients who previously consented to donate could be harmed by organ procurement causing death if they were not imminently dying but had permanently lost the capacity for awareness. How one responds to this question may depend on whether one accepts a whole-brain or higher-brain (cortical) definition of death. In Section 8, I discuss the experience of patients in the last hours, days, or weeks of their lives and how different psychological and pharmacological interventions could be justified to mitigate or prevent pain and suffering. These include meditation, hypnosis, and hallucinogens that alter consciousness, and sedation and anesthesia that diminish or suppress it. The effects of these interventions on awareness must be weighed against whether patients want to interact with others until they die. I briefly summarize the general normative aspects of consciousness in the concluding Section 9 and reiterate that the value or disvalue of consciousness depends on the relation between mind, brain, body, and environment.

## 2 The Neurobiology of Consciousness

Neurologists and cognitive neuroscientists distinguish two components of consciousness: arousal (wakefulness, alertness, vigilance) and awareness of self and surroundings.[20] The first component refers to the *level* or *state* of consciousness, and the second refers to the *content* of consciousness.[21] This definition is slightly misleading because there can be varying levels of awareness, and these can have variable effects on its content. "The content of consciousness is the substrate upon which levels of consciousness act. This content includes all the various types of information processed by hierarchically organized sensory, motor, emotional and memory systems in the brain."[22] Arousal and awareness involve lower and higher levels of information processing and responsiveness to stimuli. Arousal is mediated by the upper brain stem ascending reticular activating system (ARAS) and projections from it to the thalamus. Awareness is mediated by the ARAS, thalamus, and projections from brainstem and intralaminar thalamic nuclei to the cerebral cortex. Thalamocortical and corticocortical connectivity and communication are necessary to generate and sustain awareness.

Anesthetics cause temporary suppression of arousal and awareness by disrupting communication between the ARAS, thalamus, and cortex. Loss of arousal and awareness in coma is caused by widespread bilateral damage to the cortex or lesions in the upper brainstem and medial diencephalon.[23] Disruption or deactivation of corticocortical communication in frontoparietal networks can cause impaired awareness or unconsciousness.[24] Deactivation of these cortical networks is sufficient for loss of awareness. Cholinergic mechanisms in the prefrontal cortex seem to have a critical role in regulating the level of consciousness.[25] This implies that upper brainstem or thalamic activity alone is not sufficient to maintain it.[26]

Four of the most influential theories of consciousness have been the neural synchronization theory (NST), the global workspace theory (GWT), the integrated information theory (IIT), and the temporospatial theory of consciousness (TTC). According to NST, consciousness arises from the synchronization of dynamic and fluctuating rhythms of neural activity.[27] According to GWT, information processed in isolated unconscious modules is "broadcast" into a mental workspace that spreads across multiple cognitive systems. The theory was originally described in psychological terms[28] and later in neuroscientific terms.[29] Consciousness results from the activity of excitatory neurons in widely distributed neural networks. These include prefrontal, cingulate, and parietal cortices as well as thalamocortical loops. According to IIT, "a physical system has subjective experience to the extent that it is capable of integrating information."[30] For the brain to generate consciousness, it must functionally integrate information from specialized modules in distributed brain regions. Thalamocortical and corticocortical systems are critical for the information integration allowing awareness.[31] According to TTC, our brains exist in time and space, and these dimensions of the brain mediate awareness. Georg Northoff argues that something is conscious if its internal state can represent and track the state of its environment through space and over a wide range of timescales.[32] "Why do we have the capacity to feel and thus for sentience? Because our brain continuously integrates the different inputs from body and environment within its own ongoing temporo-spatial matrix. Our brain is temporo-spatial and hence neuro-ecological and neurobodily, which provides the capacity to feel, i.e., sentience."[33]

One example of TTC is musical experience. We respond to notes or chords on shorter timescales. We respond to refrains or choruses on longer timescales. When they are processed together, these temporal modalities result in the experience of melody.[34] The brain is wired to perceive and process these timescales, and this influences how we perceive them at a conscious level in listening to music. Similarly, neural structures enable one to perceive oneself as persisting through space and time as the same individual. Yet while they require a neural substrate, these experiences are not reducible to and thus cannot be completely explained in terms of it. They are emergent properties of neural processing rather than intrinsic properties of this processing itself. As I explain in the next six sections, this point has implications for ethical assessments of conscious and unconscious states and transitions from the first to the second, and vice versa.

The idea of integration is central to IIT and TTC, and I use both theories as the neuroscientific basis of my discussion of the ethics of consciousness. TTC is particularly relevant because it can link descriptive and normative dimensions of brain and mind. Both neural and mental properties are grounded in the same temporospatial framework. It is also relevant because prolonged DOCs and dissociation can be characterized as temporospatial disorders.

What NST, GWT, IIT, and TTC have in common is that they describe consciousness as a graded property.[35] As the degree of information integration in the brain increases, consciousness emerges. As the degree of integration decreases, consciousness fades.[36] The NCCs are neither fully on (activated) nor off (deactivated) but maintain a resting potential prior to their inhibitory or excitatory activity. Their activation or inhibition can affect the phenomenology and content of awareness and its positive or negative effects on the subject.

As an emergent property of integrated information in brainstem, subcortical and cortical systems, awareness is more than the sum of these systems.[37] There is no single region in which the neural information associated with awareness is aggregated. "Experience does not arise out of computation"[38] but from dynamic patterns of oscillation and synchronization in neural assemblies distributed throughout the brain. The idea that experience arises from these patterns suggests that it is not located in the brain. Consciousness is a feature of a constitutive, or nested, multilevel neural hierarchy. Brain and mind are two levels of a unified system. More complex regions of the central nervous system interact with less complex regions in generating and maintaining awareness. Cortical regions (frontoparietal) of the brain are more complex than subcortical (thalamus, upper brainstem) regions in the sense that they mediate a broader range of sensorimotor, cognitive, and affective processes.[39] "When higher, more complex levels are added to and interact with the lower levels, the system as a whole acquires new or even novel (never-before-existing) features."[40] Awareness is just such a feature. Disrupted communication between these levels can result in altered consciousness or unconsciousness.

Slow cortical potentials (SCPs) of electrical activity are generated by large neural assemblies in thalamocortical and corticocortical systems. NCCs and SCPs are part of the neural activity underlying awareness. But they cannot account for the specificity of the content of awareness.[41] Nor can they account for first-person experience.[42] Electroencephalography (EEG) and functional neuroimaging measuring blood flow and glucose metabolism in the brain can display NCCs and SCPs but cannot directly capture the phenomenology or content of awareness.

Patients in a VS with arousal but no awareness may not be able to feel pain or suffer from their condition. Wakeful but nonresponsive patients may be spared from these types of harm. They could still be harmed by the deprivation of experience and meaningful mental and physical activities it would have allowed. But experienced harms are worse than those we cannot experience because they adversely affect us directly. Among the ethical questions this point raises is whether patients in the MCS are better or worse off than those in the VS. These are some examples of how arousal and awareness figure in moral assessments of consciousness.

## 3 Phenomenal and Access Consciousness

Ned Block distinguishes "phenomenal consciousness" from "access consciousness."[43] He defines the first as "experience" and says that "the phenomenally conscious aspect of a state is what it is like to be in that state."[44] "Access consciousness" refers to the cognitive and sensorimotor capacity for information processing and its "availability for use in reasoning and rationally guiding speech and action."[45] This includes the cognitive and motor ability to report one's experience to others. Phenomenal consciousness seems more neurologically and psychologically fundamental than access consciousness since the ability to report one's experience presupposes that one has this experience. Yet without a report or other behavioral evidence, there may be no way of knowing whether an individual is aware. This is especially problematic among patients who become aware during surgery or are behaviorally nonresponsive from brain injury. The ontological and epistemological aspects of awareness appear to be intertwined. These two aspects are critical for determining the nature and extent of benefit and harm from having or lacking awareness, as well as responsibility for actions in states of partial or altered awareness.

Using functional magnetic resonance imaging (fMRI), Adrian Owen and other investigators have shown that some behaviorally nonresponsive patients with brain injuries may be covertly aware despite lacking the ability to report it. Activation in cortical regions of the brain when a patient was given verbal instructions to imagine performing certain actions confirmed that they responded to the instructions and were in fact aware.[46] But this activation is not the same as a report from the patient or what it is like to be aware. Nor does it reveal the content of awareness. Many severely brain-injured patients have cognitive motor dissociation (CMD). Although they are aware and have many intact cognitive functions, they lack the motor functions necessary to communicate their experience.[47] If they feel pain or suffer from it and their inability to communicate, then they may be harmed by having phenomenal consciousness without access consciousness. Imaging identifying brain regions mediating access consciousness rendered inactive from injury could lead to interventions that could restore the capacity to form and execute action plans and communicate. This would be an important component of functional recovery.

Patients who awaken during surgery cannot indicate that they are aware. Neuromuscular blocking drugs and intubation prevent them from moving and speaking. They could suffer not just from pain or panic in response to the experience but also from the inability to report it. This is another example of how phenomenal consciousness without access consciousness can result in harm from becoming aware without the ability to indicate that one is aware. Access consciousness giving patients the ability to report their experience to physicians in this and other circumstances may allow interventions to prevent or mitigate harm.

Those with irreversible conditions at the end of life may have both phenomenal and access consciousness impaired or suppressed by opioids or sedatives. These agents can relieve pain and suffering but also prevent patients from interacting with their families. The value of consciousness in enabling this interaction must be weighed against its disvalue in allowing aversive experience. Is it worse to feel pain than to be deprived of positive experiences that cannot be separated from pain? This depends on the patient's preferences. They may not be able to express these preferences while in a diminished or altered state of consciousness but may have expressed them earlier in an advance directive. Even with such a directive, the patient's preferences may have changed since they formally expressed them. Yet they may lack the access consciousness necessary to report this change and be adversely affected by physicians not acting in accord with their preferences. These examples illustrate the moral significance of phenomenal and access consciousness and the connection between them.[48]

## 4 Anesthesia and Intraoperative Awareness

Anesthesia is pharmacologically induced loss of consciousness. It causes unconsciousness by suppressing neural mechanisms mediating arousal and awareness. The effects of general anesthesia in patients undergoing surgery have shed light on the brain regions mediating consciousness. The rapid transition from consciousness to unconsciousness from anesthesia and the gradual transition from the second state back to the first when anesthetic effects diminish have further elucidated the NCCs.[49] More specifically, anesthetics cause unconsciousness by disrupting and deactivating thalamocortical and corticocortical connections and the integration of information in these brain regions. Consciousness returns when these connections are reactivated and information in these neural networks is reintegrated.[50]

Some patients become aware intraoperatively despite receiving general anesthesia. Intraoperative awareness (IA) is the experience of sensory perceptions during surgery.[51] This may involve explicit recall of awareness after surgery. Why some patients recall this experience and others do not may be a function of the extent to which the hippocampus is activated in encoding and consolidating information when the patient becomes aware. Anesthetics and sedatives cause amnesia by disrupting memory consolidation. This explains why some patients who become aware during surgery report no memory of it. In painful outpatient procedures such as colonoscopy, physicians administer intravenous analgesia to induce conscious sedation. This has the secondary effect of blocking consolidation of a memory of the patient's experience during the procedure. Despite remaining conscious, the patient later has no recall of her colonoscopy experience. IA may be due to underdosing of an anesthetic such as isoflurane or propofol or a sedative such as midazolam, or to falling concentrations of these drugs during or near the end of surgery. Postoperative memory of awareness results from the failure of anesthetics to block consolidation of information associated with awareness. Those at risk of IA typically have cardiovascular or other conditions that limit the dose of the anesthetic administered to them.

IA is difficult to prevent and detect because of the incomplete knowledge of the effects of anesthesia on neural networks generating and sustaining consciousness.[52] Depending on the concentration of the drug, some anesthetized or sedated patients can be awakened and follow commands in the isolated forearm technique without recalling it.[53] While recall of unintended awareness can increase harm postoperatively, the main source of harm is IA itself.

The incidence of IA is rare, occurring in 1–2 per 1,000 cases. The incidence of death from complications associated with general anesthesia is 1–2 per 200,000 cases.[54] But the adverse short- and long-term psychological effects of IA on patients are significant. Patients reporting that they became aware describe it as a frightening experience of pain, panic, and complete loss of control. It is an example of how being conscious for even a brief period can be bad for a person in specific circumstances. Those who become aware can be traumatized from being cut and cauterized without physicians knowing this. For those who recall becoming aware after surgery, approximately 70 percent subsequently develop posttraumatic stress disorder.[55] IA with recall is therefore much worse for the patient than IA without recall. It may be possible to prevent or even erase explicit memories of IA by infusing consolidation- or reconsolidation-blocking drugs at specific times.[56] But these interventions would not prevent IA or enable a patient to report it when it occurred.

Inhaled or infused anesthesia rapidly causes unconsciousness in a dose-response manner. The reverse transition from unconsciousness to consciousness is gradual. There is a gradual reengagement of thalamocortical and corticocortical networks mediating awareness as anesthetic effects diminish.[57] It may not be clear in this process when the patient has regained the capacity to perceive and respond to pain or to experience fear, anxiety, or panic. The fact that patients undergoing general surgery are often given a neuromuscular blocking agent causing paralysis to prevent them from moving can exacerbate these experiences. This also precludes them from indicating that they are aware to anesthesiologists and surgeons. Phenomenal consciousness without access consciousness can cause them to suffer not only from awakening and feeling pain but also from their inability to report their experience.

Analgesia is often administered preoperatively to prevent pain from reactivated cortical-limbic pathways in the nociceptive network during surgery. Yet even if a patient does not feel pain, waking up while intubated and paralyzed without being able to report it can be just as traumatic.[58] Similar sequelae may occur with diminishing effects of sedatives. They may result from problems in titrating a sedative or failing to deliver the dose necessary to reduce awareness and pain perception. Some neuroscientists divide pain into nociception and suffering. The first refers to the physical response to noxious stimulation. The second refers to the emotional response to the stimulation.[59] A patient who becomes aware can suffer in the absence of pain if suffering is defined as a state of increased distress associated with events perceived as threats to the person.[60]

Surgeons and anesthesiologists rely on anesthetic depth monitors to detect awareness. These monitors have significant limitations, however. The bispectral index (BIS) and end-tidal anesthetic-agent concentration (ETAC) system measure and monitor anesthetic depth from EEG recording of electrical signals on the scalp arising from the cortex. Although the depth of anesthesia correlates with the level of awareness, it is not identical to it. Because of this, and because BIS and ETAC record electrical signals in cortical but not also subcortical regions, they cannot clearly differentiate conscious from unconscious states. They are not reliable indices of IA. Subcortical regions like the thalamus and limbic system become activated before cortical regions in the transition from unconsciousness to consciousness. A more primitive conscious state mediated by subcortical structures may be present in the absence of cortical activity.[61] Because thalamocortical and corticocortical structures reengage gradually after subcortical structures, it may be difficult to know *when* a patient becomes aware, or *what* their level of awareness is. It may not be known whether the patient's level of awareness coincides with reactivation of pain networks or whether they would have a heightened emotional response to stimuli. This cannot be known without an intraoperative report from the patient.

The perturbational complexity index (PCI) is another way of recording and monitoring brain activity correlating with awareness. This involves using transcranial magnetic stimulation (TMS) to activate and record electrocortical responses to this activity. Like other indices, if PCI does not record subcortical or lower levels of cortical activity, then it may not be able to determine when a patient becomes aware after being unconscious. In addition, TMS may be too cumbersome for use in an intraoperative setting. More advanced monitors may detect low-frequency electrical waves in the brain as biomarkers distinguishing consciousness from unconsciousness. The slow-wave activity saturation rate could be combined with the anesthesia saturation rate to distinguish these states. Still, combining these two rates would not conclusively answer the question of when a patient's neural networks were reengaged enough to allow them to perceive pain and other noxious stimuli before regaining full awareness. Recording the neural correlates of awareness is not the same as knowing the content or subjective quality of awareness when a patient awakens during surgery.

The phenomenology of IA is critical in assessing whether or to what extent patients are harmed by it. Even if monitors could determine a patient's level of awareness at a specific time, they would not determine what it was like for them to feel pain, or experience anxiety, fear, or panic. These first-person aspects of awareness cannot be known objectively through electrophysiological measures. They could only be known from patients reporting them to physicians, and yet they lack the motor capacity to do this. These considerations underscore the subjective aspect of harm in these unexpected and unwanted neurological and psychological states.

CMD induced by an anesthetic, intubation, and neuromuscular blockade makes an awake patient unable to communicate their experience. Although a patient can have phenomenal consciousness without access consciousness, evidence of the latter is necessary to objectively confirm the former.[62] If a patient cannot report her experience to the anesthesiologist, surgeon, and others in the operating theater, then, given the limitations of anesthetic depth monitors, they cannot know whether she is aware. They may know this if a patient recalls her experience and reports it postoperatively. This is very different from what occurs intraoperatively. These considerations suggest that phenomenal consciousness without access consciousness can be worse for a patient than the absence of both types of consciousness. A patient without either type of consciousness cannot feel pain or suffer. A patient with phenomenal but not access consciousness may suffer not only from their painful and emotionally charged experience but also, and for a longer period, because of their inability to report it. Harm from CMD can also occur in patients with prolonged DOCs, which I discuss in the next section.

Suppose that a patient awakens during surgery. He cannot report this or any pain he feels because he is intubated and temporarily paralyzed with his eyes shut. From the cortical activity detected by BIS or ETAC, it is not evident to the anesthesiologist and surgeon that he is aware. Postoperatively, he does not recall being aware and does not report it to his physicians. Has he been harmed? Because becoming aware defeats his desire and expectation to remain unconscious and not feel pain or panic intraoperatively, he clearly has been harmed. Similarly, the patient undergoing the colonoscopy with conscious sedation who felt pain and suffered from the experience would have been harmed, even though she did not recall it.

If a patient with general anesthesia who becomes aware cannot report the experience to physicians, then he would be harmed for the duration of the surgery. Phenomenal consciousness without access consciousness would be worse for him. If the patient somehow was able to indicate this during surgery and it was stopped, then he would have been harmed for a shorter period. Having an explicit memory of the experience would increase the harm. But the absence of a memory of what occurred intraoperatively would not eliminate or diminish the harm when he was aware. The problem with assessing how the patient was affected in this case is that the moral issue of harm depends on the epistemic issue of knowing that he was aware. Yet the only objective evidence for this would be a report from the patient or an anesthetic depth monitor indicating cortical activity associated with awareness when the patient awakened. Neither of these indices would be available in the case I have described. There is an epistemic gap between the patient's experience and objective evidence for it. Without access consciousness, it is not clear whether this gap could be closed.

Unless a patient requests the information preoperatively, there is no defensible reason for informing a patient of the probability of IA. Because it is rare and, except possibly for high-risk surgical patients, cannot be predicted, anesthesiologists would not be obligated to mention the risk of IA in obtaining informed consent from the patient. Providing this information may undermine their obligation of nonmaleficence by making the patient anxious before surgery. There are reasonable limits to the amount of information a patient needs to consent to a procedure. Unnecessary information about a relatively low-risk procedure may have adverse psychological effects. But this must be weighed against the possible realization of the risk in significant neurological and psychological sequelae. Risk is assessed in a patient-specific manner. The key issues in preventing intraoperative and postoperative harm are identifying high-risk patients and infusing the right dose of an anesthetic or sedative to prevent IA. Anesthesiologists could identify biomarkers in thalamocortical and corticocortical networks from which to predict how anesthesia or sedation would affect arousal and awareness in individual patients. They could use these biomarkers to administer the precise dose of the drug to each patient. This could induce and sustain unconsciousness without compromising cardiorespiratory function.

## 4.1 Priming and Postoperative Effects

There are different ways of mitigating harm to patients who awaken during surgery. Analgesia can prevent or reduce pain perception. Anxiolytics such as benzodiazepines can reduce the level of anxiety from becoming aware unexpectedly. In addition, an anesthesiologist could use a priming technique by uttering certain words and making suggestions before and during surgery to modulate the patient's emotional response to becoming aware. It could also attenuate the emotional content of a memory a patient may form and store from this experience. Priming involves implicit memory occurring outside awareness. Robert Veselis defines implicit memory as a "more primitive memory system than the episodic memory system."[63] It is "learning without awareness," or "subliminal learning."[64] Priming consists in exposing a subject to a stimulus that influences a response to a later stimulus without the subject being aware of it.[65] Implicit memories of events occurring before and during surgery can be formed and stored even when a patient is unconscious. Although it is more difficult to confirm than explicit (conscious) memory, implicit memory must be factored into moral assessments of patients' postoperative mental states, behavior, and well-being.

The effects of priming cannot be predicted because it operates at an unconscious level. While implicit and explicit memories are different systems, each can influence a person's thought and action. Priming could be a nonpharmacological way of preventing panic or reducing anxiety in some patients who become aware because they can tolerate only a lower dose of an anesthetic. Perceptual priming refers to the form of the stimulus. Conceptual priming refers to the meaning of the stimulus. The first type can occur in the absence of conscious awareness under anesthesia.[66] One study has shown that therapeutic suggestions through earphones during surgery with general anesthesia can significantly reduce postoperative pain and opioid use compared with controls.[67] Nevertheless, the pain and panic from waking up on the operating table may be refractory to analgesia, anxiolytics, and priming. A traumatic memory of these experiences may be refractory to these same interventions. The limited effects of these interventions underscore the importance of preventing IA.

Priming may be have unintended negative effects in anesthetized patients. Negative perceptual priming occurring preoperatively or intraoperatively may cause psychological sequelae and adverse behavioral changes in patients following surgery. Both implicit positive and implicit aversive memory appear to involve the same neural network consisting of the hippocampus, amygdala, and neocortex. Animal studies have shown correlations between low doses of anesthesia and aversive implicit memory.[68] Studies in humans have shown that the adverse effects of this type of memory on behavior provide another reason to "avoid inadequate anaesthesia."[69] As an aversive form of perceptual priming, careless or deliberately offensive comments about a patient's body, race, or ethnicity by a surgeon or anesthesiologist while a patient is unconscious may have a negative impact on the patient's subsequent behavior if they form an implicit memory of them. Because their source cannot be detected intraoperatively, these negative outcomes cannot be known until they occur. Even if a patient remained unconscious throughout the surgery, this would not prevent an implicit aversive memory from forming and being stored because this occurs on an unconscious level. The only way to prevent this memory would be to avoid any comments or suggestions that generate it.

Although the authors of the 2020 study cited previously focused on reduced postoperative pain and opioid use from intraoperative therapeutic suggestions, they also noted that patients' perceptions of sounds and conversations could have adverse psychological effects if they retained an implicit memory of them. Accordingly, "surgeons and anaesthetists should be careful about background noise and conversations during surgery."[70] The positive and negative effects of preoperative and intraoperative perceptual priming should be included in surgeons' and anesthetists' obligations of beneficence and non-maleficence to patients.[71] These are in addition to the obligation to obtain informed consent and protect patients from potential harm associated with surgical risk.

Anesthesia-induced unconsciousness is intended to prevent awareness that would allow pain and emotional distress in patients undergoing surgery. But an insufficient dose or duration of an anesthetic may fail to disrupt neural networks mediating consciousness and allow what it is intended to prevent. The content of consciousness in this situation has disvalue for the patient. When patients remain unconscious for the duration of surgery, priming and other techniques affecting their implicit memory may have positive or negative effects on their subsequent behavior. Preoperative events surrounding patients when they are conscious, and intraoperative events occurring when they are unconscious, can affect them postoperatively. These pertain to what anesthesiologists and surgeons say or refrain from explicitly saying or suggesting before and during surgery. Caution in how they use language must be included in their professional duty to protect patients from harm.

## 5 Prolonged Disorders of Consciousness

Traumatic brain injury (TBI) or anoxia/hypoxia of the brain can result in coma. Some comatose patients eventually lose all integrated brain functions and are declared brain-dead. Others regain full consciousness, usually within two to four weeks after brain injury. Still others progress from coma to the VS, in which they show arousal and have sleep–wake cycles but are unaware of themselves and their surroundings. The VS has also been described as "unresponsive wakefulness syndrome" (UWS).[72] The 1994 Multi-Society Task Force on persistent vegetative state (PVS) concluded that a PVS would become a permanent VS three months after an anoxic injury or twelve months after a TBI.[73] More specifically, the PVS is a diagnosis, the permanent VS is a prognosis, where the probable recovery of awareness is minuscule.

Subsequent studies of these patients suggest that the second time threshold for TBI patients was overly pessimistic. They suggest that this threshold could be extended to more than a year beyond the Task Force conclusion for this prognosis to be valid.[74] Some patients in a PVS progress to a MCS. This is "a condition of severely altered consciousness characterized by minimal but definite behavioural evidence of self or environmental awareness."[75] Recovery from the MCS is defined as the "re-emergence of a functional communication system or restoration of the ability to use objects in a functional manner."[76] Whereas VS patients have lost thalamocortical and corticocortical connections, some of these connections are preserved in MCS patients. This may explain why they "retain the capacity for cognitive processing."[77]

The VS and MCS are prolonged, or chronic, DOCs.[78] They are disorders of awareness. It is either lacking, as in the VS, or intermittent, as in the MCS. They are distinct from temporary DOCs, such as absence or generalized tonic-clonic seizures in epilepsy.[79] According to some estimates, approximately 100,000 people in the United States alone are minimally conscious.[80] The Multi-Society Task Force estimated in 1994 that approximately 25,000 patients in the United States were in the VS. But subsequent data point to a much smaller prevalence, due in part to the identification of the MCS as a distinct diagnostic category in 2002. My discussion of ethical issues in the remainder of this section focuses on prolonged DOCs.

## 5.1 Experimental Interventions for DOCs

Different interventions have been tested in patients with DOCs to induce recovery of awareness and cognitive and motor functions. These include drugs such as the GABAergic receptor agonist zolpidem and the N-methyl-D-aspartate (NMDA) receptor antagonist amantadine. One placebo-controlled clinical trial tested the effects of zolpidem in fifteen patients who had been in a VS or MCS for at least one month following TBI or non-TBI. One patient transitioned from the VS to the MCS. But there was no significant difference in response between zolpidem and placebo in the remaining fourteen patients.[81] In a different study, amantadine resulted in functional improvement in some patients with DOCs following TBI.[82] But the degree of recovery was limited.

Neuromodulating techniques are therapeutic options for some of these patients, though their efficacy may depend on the extent of preserved brain function and the technique used.[83] Transcranial magnetic stimulation (TMS), repetitive transcranial magnetic stimulation (rTMS), and transcranial direct current stimulation (tDCS) penetrate the cortex but nòt the thalamus and thus cannot activate thalamocortical connections necessary to restore awareness and cognitive capacities. A randomized double-blind clinical trial testing the effects of high-frequency rTMS over the left dorsolateral prefrontal cortex showed that it did not improve cognition in patients with TBI.[84]

Deep brain stimulation (DBS) may be an effective neuromodulating technique in promoting cognitive and motor recovery from DOCs because of its ability to directly target neural pathways mediating cognitive and motor capacities.[85] These include the capacity to communicate, the loss of which is one of the main sources of suffering in these patients.[86] DBS may induce axonal regeneration in brain regions that have been damaged and dysfunctional for an extended period. This technique may improve capacities that have been impaired following TBI. But it may not have this same potential in patients with anoxic or hypoxic injury and extensive axonal damage.

The first Food and Drug Administration (FDA) approved clinical trial of DBS for a patient in the MCS was conducted in 2006–07. It resulted in restoration of some motor and cognitive functions in a patient who had been in this state for six years following an assault.[87] This included verbal ability that allowed some, albeit limited, communication.[88] The trial tested the hypothesis that electrical stimulation of the central thalamus could modulate the mesocircuit consisting of the thalamus, basal ganglia, and frontal cortex and enable some degree of functional recovery.

In the years since this trial, however, studies have not shown significant improvement from DBS for most patients with DOCs. In one of these studies, fourteen patients in the VS or MCS from TBI or hypoxic encephalopathy were treated with DBS of the left centromedian-parafascicular complex of the thalamus. Two of the patients regained consciousness and the ability to live independently. One patient regained consciousness but has persistent motor impairment and remains in a wheelchair. Another patient can follow simple commands. The condition of seven patients remained unchanged, and three died from causes unrelated to TBI.[89] Although ongoing and future studies may yield more positive results, the therapeutic effects of electrical brain stimulation for most DOC patients since the 2006–07 study have been limited.

Neuroimaging identifying areas of preserved axonal connectivity and somatosensory evoked potentials as targets of stimulation could lead to functional improvement in more patients. Diffusion tensor imaging and algorithmic EEG have been used in one study to accurately predict the extent of chronic neurodegeneration in people with TBI.[90] By detecting these and other biomarkers of neural function in a patient-specific manner, researchers could identify which patients would be more or less likely to respond to neurostimulation and have significant functional recovery. This would allow researchers to exclude patients with diffuse axonal injury from clinical trials testing DBS to restore or increase awareness and cognitive and motor capacities. In addition to not exposing patients to any risk of harm in these trials, this exclusion could also reduce the risk of families consenting on behalf of brain-injured patients based on unreasonable expectations about the therapeutic potential of the research. Still, among those with less diffuse injury and some preserved thalamocortical and corticocortical connectivity, predicting how patients would respond to neurostimulation and whether it would allow them to transition from intermittent to full awareness and functional independence is fraught with uncertainty.

Whether neurostimulation could induce neural regeneration resulting in functional restoration would depend on the extent of injury and preserved neural connectivity. Without some preserved connectivity, DBS or other techniques would not be able to supplement or compensate for neural deficits. Neuromodulation would probably cease as soon as the technique was discontinued. Extensive loss of neural connectivity would preclude a therapeutic outcome. The prognosis for patients with this loss would be poor.

In 2019, researchers reported that an implant delivering electrical stimulation to an area of the brain of a woman with a TBI from an automobile accident eighteen years earlier restored many of her neural functions.[91] She can perform many of the same cognitive and motor tasks she performed before her injury. Among other activities, she is reading novels and lives independently. The variability of outcomes of DBS for brain-injured patients warrants caution in making claims about whether the therapeutic potential of this technique will be realized in many patients with disability from severe brain injury. This variability reflects differences in the extent of injury among patients and the degree of plasticity in their brains. Currently, the number of DOC patients who experience significant recovery from DBS is low. But this case illustrates that careful selection of patients with more intact neural connectivity and more effective neurostimulation may result in greater functional recovery and independence for them. This may include not only DBS but also less invasive ultrasonic thalamic stimulation, which has resulted in significant improvement in two MCS patients.[92]

One explanation for inconclusive outcomes of these treatment studies is that patients are typically classified by diagnostic syndrome (e.g., VS or MCS). This is a categorical limitation because different mechanisms of brain injury (e.g., trauma, hypoxia, ischemia) and different focal and multi-focal locations of brain damage can produce the same diagnostic syndrome. Yet syndromic diagnosis involves a heterogeneous group of research subjects. Because each brain injury is unique and involves a different pathophysiology and lesion location, including all these patients in one category leads to inconclusive study results.

There are other challenges in conducting clinical trials testing DBS for the MCS and VS. Because neural responses to neurostimulation depend on a certain degree of preserved neural function, and because many patients with DOCs do not meet this threshold, the number of patients enrolled in these trials generally has been small. This can affect the statistical significance of outcomes of these trials. In addition, researchers selecting subjects for a placebo-controlled trial may not be able to discriminate between patients who could recover from neurostimulation and those who would recover spontaneously.[93] This could be especially problematic if the trial included patients in an MCS or VS two years after brain injury because spontaneous recovery often occurs within this period. It could complicate assessing the efficacy of DBS for this patient population. Neural biomarkers that might predict recovery could be similar in patients receiving and those not receiving neurostimulation. Enrolling patients who have had DOCs for five years or more after brain injury might avoid this problem. But it could result in losing a therapeutic opportunity before the progression of neurodegeneration from the injury. Still, the case of the woman who regained functional independence from neurostimulation eighteen years after a TBI suggests that the therapeutic window for neuroregeneration and neurorestoration may remain open indefinitely. Again, though, this would depend on the degree of preserved brain function, as well as whether DBS could activate neuroplastic mechanisms. These considerations point to the varying natural history of DOCs.[94] Many patients with these disorders improve spontaneously, especially after TBI. The details of the injury and how recently or remotely it occurs are essential in determining statistical prognosis.

Most patients with DOCs lack the decisional capacity to consent to participate in research. Families or other substitute decision-makers can give proxy consent for them to be enrolled in a clinical trial. Many of these patients would be excluded from research because extensive brain damage from TBI or anoxic injury would make it unlikely that their brains would respond to stimulation. It would not be unfair to exclude these patients from research if they could not contribute to assessing the safety and efficacy of DBS or other techniques to improve or restore neural function. For those with enough preserved function making them candidates for research, some families may be reluctant to give proxy consent for a patient to participate in a placebo-controlled trial because they could be assigned to the control arm with no intervention, or a "sham" intervention. This may reflect a therapeutic misconception and a belief that a clinical trial will restore function in a particular patient, ignoring the fact that the purpose of the trial is to determine the safety and efficacy of an experimental intervention for a group of research subjects.[95] Because of their desire for the patient to improve, they may not duly consider that, if the trial demonstrated that DBS could restore a significant degree of awareness and cognitive and motor functions, then eventually those in the control arm would receive it as well. But substitute decision-makers would prefer to see improvement sooner rather than later. Others may be motivated to give proxy consent by the belief or hope that the technique was a last resort for functional improvement that would provide some relief from their caregiving burden and associated distress. This may be more likely to occur the longer the patient had been in an MCS and dependent on others. These are among the "logistical and methodological difficulties of conducting placebo-controlled trials in this population."[96]

Policies must be in place to protect nonresponsive patients with DOCs who would be vulnerable research subjects. Their vulnerability involves not only the risk of intracranial hemorrhage, infection, and inflammation from implanted electrodes in DBS but also their inability to consider these risks and consent to participate in the research. Protections would include minimizing risk from intervening in a damaged brain and ensuring that families or others consenting for a patient to participate in a placebo-controlled trial understood the design and purpose of the trial. Investigators would have to ensure that, by allowing a patient to be a research subject, substitute decision-makers would be doing what the patient would have wanted and decided if she had this capacity. They would have to ensure that others acted in the patient's best interests.[97]

## 5.2 Normative Assessment of DOCs

Is it better to be minimally conscious than vegetative?[98] This is not just a neurological question but also a philosophical and psychological question about well-being and the level of mental and physical functional capacity in terms of which it is measured.[99] Because these states involve cognitive and motor impairment (MCS), or loss of awareness and cognition (VS), it may be more appropriate to ask whether one is worse than the other. The relevant comparison is not just between the neurological states of these patients but also between their psychological states, or lack thereof in the VS patient. This question may strike some as incoherent because a severely neurologically compromised patient does not have the capacity to compare what being minimally conscious would be like with what being vegetative would be like.[100] A minimally conscious patient may not have the capacity to compare her current state with an earlier state in which she was awake but unaware or awake and fully aware. We cannot know objectively what it is like subjectively for a nonresponsive patient to be aware. Yet it is coherent to objectively compare the lives of two distinct patients in these two states based on neurological features and the capacity or incapacity for experience and cognitive and motor functions.

Although the vegetative patient has more extensive neurological injury, he is not aware of his condition and cannot suffer from being aware of it. Also, a vegetative patient may lack the capacity to feel pain if the injury has damaged the pain network in his brain. There may be variability in this capacity, depending on how extensive the injury is.[101] In contrast, a minimally conscious patient may be aware of her cognitive and motor impairment and retain the nociceptive network in her brain's "pain matrix," which can cause her to experience pain.[102] Some patients diagnosed as vegetative have indicated that they feel pain by changing neural activity in response to questions from investigators, as measured by fMRI.[103] This suggests a level of awareness corresponding to the MCS rather than the VS and thus a misdiagnosis. Many DOC patients with some level of awareness cannot communicate that they are in pain because of motor impairment and CMD. Accordingly, "aggressive pain management should always be initiated for patients in MCS, as their capacity for subjective awareness of pain is preserved."[104] But analgesia cannot prevent suffering from awareness of functional impairment, dependence on others, and the inability to communicate with physicians and family. In these psychological respects, a minimally conscious patient may be worse off than a vegetative one.

An MCS patient with some preserved axonal connectivity in thalamocortical and corticocortical circuits may be a candidate for DBS aimed at increasing their level of awareness and restoring functional independence. In these neuro-logical respects, an MCS patient would be better off than a VS patient. The latter would be much less likely to respond to the technique because of the greater degree of axonal injury and disrupted neural connectivity. For the MCS patient, the benefit from functional recovery could outweigh harm from pain or suffer-ing they may have experienced before stimulation. It could also outweigh the harm from memories they may have of this aversive experience. Yet restoring some functions but not others and only to a limited degree may not result in a net benefit. If the technique restored full awareness and most cognitive and motor functions, then the patient would clearly benefit. If it did not have these outcomes but increased the patient's level of awareness, then it could harm him by allowing him to feel pain and suffer from his experience of disability and dependence on others. Neurostimulation enabling a patient to progress from a lower to a higher level of awareness would not necessarily make him better off than he was before this intervention.

"Meaningful" recovery for a patient suggests a high degree of functional recovery and independence. Some investigators have noted a general 20–30 percent rate of recovery of awareness and cognitive and motor functions among MCS patients.[105] This rate includes patients who recover spontaneously and those who recover from pharmacological or neuromodulating interven-tions. There is variability in the degree of recovery among patients, and although it typically occurs within five years of brain injury, it may occur later as well. The extent to which a patient regains functions is neurologically significant when considering their previous baseline function. The relevant baseline in assessing benefit is not the MCS before DBS but normal brain function before brain injury. It is questionable whether recovery that fell far short of functional independence would be meaningful. According to one estimate, "68 percent of patients with TBI in inpatient rehabilitation services regained consciousness, and of those, close to 20 percent regained functional independence."[106] In the second group, endogenous repair and growth mechan-isms in their brains may have reactivated damaged neural connections. But the 80 percent who did not regain functional independence is a significant number. Many patients with DOCs do not recover to this level spontaneously, from psychoactive drugs, or from neurostimulation.

Even if a patient with a DOC had significant neurological recovery from DBS, this would not necessarily translate into psychological recovery of cogni-tive, affective, and volitional capacities. This depends not only on how their *brains* respond to the intervention but also on how *they* respond to its effects. In most cases, neurostimulation would not completely restore all functions but would leave some impaired. Some patients adjust to neurological and mental impairment over time.[107] Others do not, and they may be distressed by the change in their neurological and mental states. Variable outcomes of brain injury on neurological function make it difficult to predict how patients would respond neurologically and psychologically to neurostimulation.

Quality-of-life assessments are subjective and differ among neurologically compromised patients. Although what it is like to be in a state of impaired awareness cannot be measured objectively, neuroimaging techniques may enable investigators to have indirect knowledge of patients' experience. MCS patients may feel that their lives are worth living. Some may be able to express this in a primitive form of communication by activating cortical networks in response to binary questions. This can be confirmed by EEG or functional neuroimaging. Some patients with locked-in syndrome (LIS) who are fully conscious but almost completely paralyzed have been able to indicate that they have good quality of life. They have done this through eyelid movements expressing "yes" and "no" responses to investigators' questions or through cortical signals using EEG.[108]

Others may express a different attitude. Tony Nicklinson was locked in and paralyzed below the neck for seven years from a brainstem stroke when he requested to the UK Court to be allowed to end his life with the aid of a physician. The Court rejected his request just six days before he died from pneumonia at age fifty-eight. Communicating through a computer that he operated by eyelid movements, Nicklinson stated that he wanted to end his "dull, miserable, demeaning, undignified, and intolerable life."[109] These differ-ent attitudes depend not only on one's level of awareness of a neurological disorder, functional impairment, or the extent of functional recovery from interventions to treat the disorder. They also depend on the content of this awareness and how one responds to it.

"Burden" is often used interchangeably with "harm." As noted in Section 1, individuals can benefit from or be harmed by events they cannot directly experience. They can be harmed even if they have lost the capacity for con-sciousness. These judgments may be made about patients in the VS. Pippa Knight was a five-year-old girl with a profound brain injury who progressed to a PVS. She received prolonged ventilation in a pediatric intensive care unit (PICU). Because she was diagnosed as persistently rather than permanently vegetative, she had not permanently lost the capacity for awareness. A UK High Court judge reasoned that it was wrong to prolong her life, even if she had no negative experiences.[110] The judge claimed that "both her ongoing condition and her necessary treatment in the PICU constitute burdens upon her person notwithstanding her lack of conscious awareness."[111] If a persistently vegeta-tive five-year-old cannot feel pain and does not have the capacity for any interests, then it is not clear in what sense continued life-sustaining care would be a burden to her. In adults who have this capacity, even if they can be adversely affected after permanently losing the capacity for awareness, experienced harm has a more direct impact on and is more pertinent to their well-being than nonexperienced harm.

## 5.3 Communicating Wishes about Life-Sustaining Interventions

Because many MCS patients cannot effectively communicate, it can be difficult to know whether they feel pain or suffer, and whether they want to continue living in this state. Citing neurological and behavioral evidence, some commentators have responded negatively to the question of whether these patients could benefit from any actions.[112] A minimally conscious state with little or no hope of recovery would not be part of a life worth living. This judgment could support discontinuing life-sustaining artificial nutrition and hydration (ANH) and other interventions keeping them alive. Others have argued that many of these patients recover over time, and that the public should be disabused of the belief that "these disorders are hopeless and attempts to treat them futile."[113] The belief that these attempts are futile may preclude interventions that could result in significant recovery for patients with DOCs. If imaging could identify biomarkers predicting that some patients would respond to neurostimulation, then claims that the disorders are hopeless could prevent these patients from transitioning from long-term rehabilitation to independent living.

In legal cases involving disagreement between families and other parties regarding the benefits of ANH and other life-sustaining care, courts typically take the default position that life in the MCS is beneficial to the patient and that these types of care should continue.[114] When patients are unable to communicate their wishes, there may be disagreement among those making substitute judgments for them. These judgments may not accurately reflect their wishes and how they value their lives. If a patient in an MCS wanted to continue living, then continued ANH would benefit them. If they did not want to continue living, then continued ANH would harm them. The ethical point here is not just that covertly aware patients are "alive inside,"[115] but that they also may have interests in how their lives go. The inability to communicate these interests may cause them to suffer in silence.

Systems such as brain-computer interfaces (BCIs) may allow behaviorally nonresponsive patients with the requisite level of cognitive and motor capacity to produce letters and words through a language-processing system. A BCI with an intracortical array implanted in language-processing areas of the brain could decode and transmit signals associated with speech to a computer. Depending on the volume and consistency of word production, this could enable patients to reliably communicate that they were suffering and their wishes and decisions about continuing or discontinuing life-sustaining care.[116] This technique may also enable some patients to give informed consent to participate in clinical trials testing the safety and efficacy of DBS for MCS patients. This would obviate the need for proxy consent from families of nonresponsive patients and avoid situations in which they would be enrolled in this research against their wishes. But it would depend on the level of cognitive and motor function. It should be noted that the number of MCS patients who could communicate is likely very small. They may have aphasia, apraxia, dementia, and other cerebral consequences of multifocal brain damage that would limit their ability to communicate. This distinguishes them from patients with LIS and advanced amyotrophic lateral sclerosis (ALS), who are more likely able to communicate because the cerebral hemispheric function underlying this ability is intact.[117]

Some patients may have expressed a wish to others before a TBI or anoxic injury that they would not want to remain alive in a neurologically compromised and completely dependent state. This might be included formally in an advance directive or, more likely, informally in discussions with family. Some with intact cognitive functions may have changed their mind but not be able to make this clear to physicians and family because of their motor and language impairment. Communicating through a BCI could enable them to express their current attitudes and wishes and provide an accurate statement of them. Their cognitive state might include knowledge of advances in restorative interventions that were not available when they commented on not wanting to continue living in a DOC. It could ensure that others performed actions they wanted and refrained from actions they did not want. It might also provide some insight into the phenomenology of living with a prolonged disorder of consciousness.

Nevertheless, the clarity and reliability of expressing momentous decisions about life-sustaining care would require more than brain activation in response to verbal commands or "yes" or "no" responses to binary questions.[118] It would require that the patient produce a certain number of words that would be sufficiently coherent and consistent to constitute robust communication of their thoughts to physicians, families, or others whose actions would affect them. This could avoid misinterpretation of a patient's wishes or decisions from simple affirmative or negative responses to questions, or from incoherent or inconsistent word production. It would in turn prevent actions by others that were not consistent with their interests.

Reliable communication from MCS patients would depend on their cognitive, motor, and volitional capacity to effectively use the interface. This would require a high level of motivation, attention, patience, and persistence in operating it. Failure to use it for this purpose could be just as harmful to the patient as misinterpreted minimal communication. Investigators would have to select patients for BCI-mediated communication based on evidence of cognitive and motor capacity. There would still be uncertainty in whether patients had the specific capacity to translate the intention to produce letters and words into their actual production through the interface. It may seem unfair that some patients would have the opportunity to control their fate through this form of communication, while others would not. But the selection of some patients for this technique and the exclusion of others based on neurological and behavioral criteria would not be unfair. It would be a fair form of discrimination that would not be based on the character of the patients. Rather, it would be based on which areas of their brains were damaged, which were intact, and whether or to what extent these features enabled or prevented them from using a BCI to express wishes and decisions about medical care.

Although BCI-enabled communication is still at an early experimental stage, it could allow some patients to make these decisions for themselves and avoid substitute decisions by others. It would allow them to determine the care they receive "by proclamation rather than proxy."[119] This type of communication could resolve uncertainty about what some MCS or other behaviorally nonresponsive patients wanted. This could also include patients who are fully conscious but unable to speak, such as those with LIS or ALS. It would be more likely in these patients because of their intact cerebral hemispheric function. One patient fully locked-in from ALS was able to formulate and express words and sentences using a spelling interface and auditory neurofeedback training.[120] For those using a BCI for this purpose, "success will be marked by how readily our patients can share their thoughts with all of us."[121]

## 6 Dissociative Disorders

Consciousness can be disrupted or altered by different neuropsychiatric and psychological events. In epilepsy, consciousness is disrupted by abnormal electrical activity in the cerebral cortex. It can also be altered by other dysregulated mechanisms that ordinarily regulate the integration of information in the brain. This can result in dissociative disorders, where "consciousness is not fully integrated because the normal ability self-consciously to observe oneself, to be aware of and monitor oneself, is missing or severely diminished."[122] Dissociation includes somnambulism (sleepwalking) and other sleep-related disorders (parasomnias), fugue states, severe intoxication, delirium, catatonia, and other conditions.[123] While dissociative disorders may be induced by voluntary actions such as excessive alcohol intake, they often result from a combination of genetic factors, neuropsychiatric disorders, abnormal sleep physiology, sleep deprivation, and psychosocial stress.

In people with somnambulism, functional neuroimaging studies have shown abnormalities in cerebral blood flow, glucose metabolism, and rhythms in the brainstem, anterior and posterior hypothalamus, basal forebrain, ventral tegmental area, thalamus, and cortex.[124] Specifically, there is inhibition in brain regions mediating wakefulness but activation in motor areas. In one study, single- photon emission computed tomography (SPECT) showed abnormal patterns of brain activity in sleepwalkers even during wakefulness, especially after sleep deprivation.[125] While previously believed to be a disorder of arousal, the current consensus is that somnambulism is a disorder of slow-wave sleep regulation.[126]

Individuals in dissociative states are not fully conscious or unconscious but somewhere in-between. These states fall along a neuropsychological spectrum with different levels of awareness. They can impair agency to varying degrees, depending on the degree of dissociation. Whereas somnambulism can impair agency, catatonia and delirium can undermine it. Dissociative states have been described as altered states of consciousness and disconnection from the world.[127] These involve a "changed overall pattern of conscious experience," or "the subjective feeling and explicit recognition that one's own subjective experience has changed."[128] This assumes that individuals do not completely lose self-awareness in these states. Like the reemergence of consciousness following general anesthesia, dissociative states are an example of how consciousness is not always on or off but at higher or lower levels depending on excitatory and inhibitory mechanisms in the brain. Information disruption in these and other disorders can range from moderate to severe.[129] This range can determine whether or to what extent an individual in such a state could retain the capacity for behavior control to be morally and criminally responsible for their actions. The neuroethical and neurolegal issues of agency and responsibility are the common normative denominator in dissociative disorders.

The key question in normative evaluations of actions performed by individuals in dissociative states is whether the actions are intentional or automatic. Responsibility for actions presupposes that they are intentional and voluntary and thus within one's conscious control. If an action is nonintentional and nonvoluntary, then one cannot be responsible for it. Presumably, an individual acting in a dissociative state has no conscious control of the action and cannot be responsible for it because the action is automatic rather than intentional. Behavior control and responsibility come in degrees, however. In some cases, an individual may have enough intentionality for some degree of control of and responsibility for an action even if they acted in an altered conscious state. This depends on how much information they can consciously process about themselves and their environment when they act.

Amnesia is often a symptom of somnambulism. Sleepwalkers may report that they do not recall actions they performed in this state. This does not demonstrate that they lacked behavior control when they acted. Stephen Morse points out that "dissociative states are often followed by amnesia, but later amnesia does not necessarily entail that the agent lacked awareness or full intentionality during the conduct. One may be fully aware of conduct and later amnesic, and dissociated conduct may or may not be followed by amnesia."[130] Amnesia is not a mitigating or excusing condition regarding responsibility for actions. What matters in determining whether a person had enough control of their thought and behavior to be responsible for their actions is not whether they can recall them. Rather, what matters is their level of awareness at the time of the action and whether they acted intentionally. Episodic memory, the capacity to consciously recall one's experience of events, is not the critical form of memory in these cases. Recall is fallible and may not involve the same information available to the agent when they acted. Conscious prospective and working memory are necessary for the agent to form and execute intentions by holding and accessing information stored in the brain. Nonconscious procedural memory is necessary for an agent to perform motor skills associated with the bodily movement identified with the action. These capacities can be gleaned from the individual's behavior at the time of the action.

A particular dissociative state may be psychogenic or caused by a neuropsychiatric disorder involving mechanisms regulating sleep and wakefulness. It may also be induced by hallucinogens such as psilocybin and anesthetics such as ketamine. Whereas somnambulism involves a nebulous state between sleep and wakefulness, depersonalization and derealization from these drugs involve a sense of detachment from one's body or the external world. Dissociative states may be transient or extend over longer periods. They can impair executive functions and the capacity for decision-making. But there may be some degree of cognitive and volitional control of actions performed in these states and thus some degree of responsibility for them. "Dissociation is a degree phenomenon ... it lends itself to a continuum of moral ascription ranging from full responsibility to mitigation to full excuse, depending on the resulting level of rational impairment."[131]

Sleepwalking and other dissociative states are often described as forms of automatism. This is nonintentional and nonvoluntary unconscious behavior that fails to meet the *mens rea* requirement for criminal responsibility. This requirement states that a person is guilty of a criminal offense if they acted "purposely, knowingly, recklessly, or negligently, as the law may require with respect to each material element of the offense."[132] Sleepwalking can be an excusing condition if it undermines the capacity to respond to reasons for or against different actions.[133] We perform many actions automatically in completing motor tasks. But these are distinct from actions resulting from responsiveness to reasons, deliberation, planning and decision-making. Actions associated with automatism are not autonomous because a person in such a state cannot endorse the mental states from which they issue and identify them as their own.[134] They are not intentional or voluntary, not within a person's conscious control, and thus are not events for which they could be responsible. One could argue that automatism is not a form of agency.

Because they come in degrees, dissociative disorders may not completely preclude autonomous agency. As altered conscious states, dissociative states are not completely unconscious and do not involve completely automatic behavior. They are partly conscious and can be at least partly autonomous. Dissociative states may allow some capacity for planning and decision-making. I have claimed that whether sleepwalkers recall their actions in this state is not critical in determining whether they were intentional and voluntary. As part of their episodic memory, they may be able to provide a rationale for their behavior when they recall it. These accounts may not be accurate and reliable because they are recalling events associated with disrupted information in the mind and brain. Indeed, any retrospective assessment of a person's behavior in a dissociative state is problematic. "Retrospective mental state evaluations are difficult to make; but deciding how dissociated an agent was in the past can be fearsomely difficult."[135] Observing a person's behavior after an action cannot confirm the extent to which a dissociative state interfered with their reasoning and decision-making when they acted. Mental processing associated with this capacity can change over this period. A psychological assessment of an action at a later time cannot provide a conclusive explanation for the mental states that led to it at an earlier time.

Neuroimaging would not resolve this issue either. Cerebral blood flow, glucose metabolism, and rhythms in the brain are not static but constantly changing. Neural function measured by fMRI, positron emission tomography (PET), SPECT, or other imaging modalities days or even hours after an action in a dissociative state may be very different from neural function when the agent performed it. The most reliable measure in assessing whether or to what extent a person with a dissociative disorder had control of their behavior when they acted would be to reconstruct and analyze the sequence of events resulting in the action. A history of behavior with such a disorder could also be part of this assessment. Although it would be imperfect and may depend partly on the credibility of witnesses, an account of the person's actions during an episode may indicate some degree of intentionality. In that case, they could be partly responsible. The disorder may mitigate responsibility for an action or actions committed in a dissociative state. But if the actions were not completely automatic, then dissociation would not be an excuse.

## 6.1 Agency, Control, and Responsibility

Sleepwalking consists of a rare combination of abnormal deep sleep and wakeful motor behavior. It has "a high potential for serious injury and both nighttime and daytime sequelae."[136] Episodes can last from a few minutes to hours. Claims that sleepwalking is completely automatic are based on a misconception about the neurological and psychological features of this dissociative disorder. Although a somnambulistic episode can be triggered by a primary sleep disorder, such as sleep apnea or sleep deprivation, this does not imply that behavior during the episode is beyond an affected person's control. Based on studies of sleepwalkers, Antonio Zadra and coinvestigators point out that their behavior is not simply automatic but may have an underlying rationale and some degree of planning.[137]

> Although sleepwalking is often characterized in terms of its automatic behaviors, ongoing work in the phenomenology of somnambulism indicates that perceptual, cognitive and affective dimensions can play an important role in the subjective experience of adult sleepwalkers. Furthermore, some patients report that their somnambulistic behaviors are motivated by an intrinsic sense of urgency or underlying logic that explains their behaviors during episodes.[138]

This logic may not always be consistent. But the conscious cognitive and volitional aspects of their behavior may indicate some degree of intentionality and thus some control of it. It may be partly but not entirely automatic behavior.

These considerations suggest a normative assessment of mitigated rather than full responsibility or excuse for actions performed during sleepwalking. This is based on one's cognitive, affective, and volitional capacities to respond to reasons and perform some actions or refrain from performing others. By themselves, brain abnormalities correlating with sleepwalking are not normatively significant. They are significant if they impair these mental capacities and result in actions that harm oneself or others. Neuroimaging showing abnormalities in brain regions mediating inhibitory and excitatory activity underlying behavior can clarify questions about intentionality and control when the behavioral evidence is ambiguous. But the behavior itself is the most reliable basis for evaluating actions performed in dissociative states. We can draw inferences from the behavior to the presence or absence of conscious mental states in general and intentionality in particular. Two cases of sleepwalking illustrate and support this point.

More than seventy years ago, Ivy Cogdon axe-bludgeoned her nineteen-year-old daughter to death while sleepwalking. A jury found her not guilty of homicide on the grounds of noninsane automatism.[139] Michael Moore claims that Cogdon was unable to consciously access and respond to reasons for not killing her daughter. Yet he also points out that she performed "complex routines requiring perception and readjustment in order to reach certain goals."[140] Her behavior suggested that she formed and executed an intention in performing the action, even if she seemed unaware of it. Like other sleep-walkers, Cogdon may have had some degree of self-awareness and awareness of her relationship to her immediate environment. Commenting on this case, Morse states that "the movements of the unconscious agent that cause harms appear to execute more general intentions. After all, it is implausible that the harms done are random goals . . . . To execute a general intention requires that the agent *must* be aware at some level of the intention that she is trying to execute."[141]

If Cogdon formed, held, and executed an intention to kill her daughter, then she had some cognitive and volitional control of her behavior. It was not entirely automatic. This control could have been enough for her to respond to a reason to cancel the intention and refrain from killing her daughter. This control and the causal role of her intention in the action would also have been sufficient for her to meet the *mens rea* requirement for criminal responsibility, despite the jury's decision in this case.[142] The dissociative state may have warranted a judgment of partial or mitigated responsibility. But it would not have warranted an excuse.

In the early morning of May 24, 1987, Kenneth Parks rose from the couch on which he was lying and drove 23 kilometers to his parents-in-law's house. He strangled his father-in-law into unconsciousness and repeatedly stabbed his mother-in-law. He then drove to the nearest police station and said that he thought that he had killed some people. Parks' episodic memory of the events that occurred that early morning was fragmented. He recalled some events but not others. He was charged with first-degree murder of his mother-in-law, who died from her stabbing injuries. Parks pleaded not guilty, claiming that he was sleepwalking when he assaulted his in-laws. His defense claimed that his actions were the product of noninsane automatism and pointed out that he had a history of somnambulism.[143] He was found not guilty on the grounds that his fragmented episodic memory was consistent with sleepwalking, and that this was an excusing condition. This ruling was upheld by the Supreme Court of Canada.[144] Parks' impaired episodic memory in his account of events was presumed to be evidence of cognitive and volitional impairment that prevented him from controlling his actions.

Again, though, retrograde amnesia in failing to recall events surrounding one's actions is not evidence of a lack of intentionality and responsiveness to reasons when one acted. Parks' amnesia did not confirm that strangling and stabbing his in-laws was nonintentional and automatic. The main flaw in the legal reasoning about this case was the judgment that somnambulism always involves completely automatic behavior. Based on SPECT imaging showing deactivation in the frontoparietal cortex and activation in the limbic anterior cingulate cortex in sleepwalkers, one study showed that there was a "dissociation between body sleep and mind sleep."[145] It appears that, during a somnambulistic episode, a person "experiences motor arousal without mental arousal."[146] This seems to support automatism. But perceptual, cognitive, and affective processes may be active in addition to motor processes in sleepwalkers. If these processes are active, then the behavior is not entirely automatic.

Motor arousal is associated with procedural memory, the ability to perform learned motor skills.[147] This is a nondeclarative form of memory that operates outside of conscious awareness. Some of Parks' behavior leading to his criminal acts could be explained in terms of motor arousal and procedural and spatial memory in knowing where his in-laws lived and how to drive there. Spatial memory may be conscious or unconscious, depending on the context of action. But these two types of memory alone would not be sufficient to explain Parks' criminal acts. The sequence of events in which he got into his car, drove to his in-laws' house, and attacked them suggests some degree of planning and thus some degree of intentionality. His behavior included unconscious and conscious components. It was at least partly goal-directed and as such partly within his cognitive and volitional control.

Complex behaviors defy straightforward explanations. The sequence of events leading to and resulting in Parks' attack on his in-laws suggests that his behavior was not entirely automatic. This conflicts with the Canadian Supreme Court's judgment of excuse based on noninsane automatism. In addition to the cognitive capacity to respond to reasons and form an intention to act, one must have the volitional capacity to execute the intention in the action to be responsible for it. The outcome in this case suggested that Parks had and exercised both capacities, which would indicate some degree of control of his behavior and justify an attribution of partial criminal responsibility. The dissociative state and lack of complete cognitive control of his behavior were a mitigating but not an excusing condition.

Functional neuroimaging can reveal the dysregulated neural mechanisms of somnambulism and other dissociative disorders. But the connection between this dysregulation and dissociative mental states is not completely understood.[148] Advances in neuroimaging could clarify this connection, and brain abnormalities associated with somnambulism could be an excusing condition in specific cases. But they would excuse only if they undermined the capacity for intentionality and responsiveness to reasons for or against different actions. The abnormalities would have to be significant, and impairment in the relevant mental capacities would have to manifest in the person's behavior at the time of action. As noted, even if neuroimaging showed significant abnormalities in perfusion, metabolism, and neural rhythms, these functions may change over time. Imaging could not determine whether these abnormalities were present, or the extent to which they were present, when the person acted. Depending on how they affect a person's mental states, neural function and dysfunction may correlate with varying degrees of control of thought and behavior at different times.

In cases where somnambulism entailed a high risk of self-harm and harm to others, an affected person may be advised by neurologists and psychologists to avoid sleep deprivation. This can trigger sleepwalking episodes. They may also be prescribed certain medications or participate in cognitive behavioral therapy to prevent or reduce the risk of having them. If an individual failed to heed this advice and refused to accept these interventions, then they could be responsible for actions committed in a dissociative state. This claim could be based on the affected person's negligence. If the interventions were safe and effective and not unduly burdensome, then it would not be unreasonable to expect the person to accept them. Being incapacitated because of dissociation would not necessarily excuse them for actions committed in that state if they had some control over events that triggered it.[149] Although the person partly or even completely lacked cognitive and volitional control when they acted, they had cognitive control before the episode in knowing the likely consequences of failing to take measures that could have prevented dissociation. They could be responsible for nonintentional and nonvoluntary actions because of this failure.

These considerations about sleepwalking are similar to the normative assessment of a person acting in a voluntarily induced intoxicated, psychotic, or otherwise altered conscious state. For example, in ketamine- or psilocybin-induced dissociation outside of a clinical or research setting, one could avoid being in such a state with the associated incapacities by not taking these drugs. Voluntarily taking them and the cognitive control in knowing that one could become mentally or physically incapacitated could make one morally and criminally responsible for any harmful actions committed in this state.

Cognitive control could make responsibility transfer from the earlier to the later time.[150] A diachronic account of the sequence of events resulting in a harmful act could show that acting in a dissociated state with only partial awareness may not be an excusing condition regarding that act.[151] A neurological disorder like somnambulism can be an excusing or mitigating condition depending on the extent to which it impairs the mental capacities necessary for responsibility. But an individual with such a disorder may have enough of these capacities to be partly responsible for their actions.

Dissociative disorders alter consciousness and can impair behavior control. But people with these disorders may retain some capacity to form and execute intentions in voluntary actions. Whether or to what extent actions performed in a dissociative state are intentional or automatic can be assessed by examining the behavior of those who commit them. Imaging can confirm neurological dysfunction underlying these disorders. But it will not decisively show that a person had or lacked the mental capacity to control their behavior. In cases of severe disruption of consciousness and incapacity, some individuals may nonetheless be responsible for actions committed in these states if they are induced by voluntary use of psychoactive drugs, or if they result from failure to take reasonable measures to prevent them.

The effects of dissociative disorders are variable and can occur at different times. Some behaviors can be both partly intentional and partly automatic, partly conscious and partly unconscious involving different but complementary cognitive and motor functions. They can affect behavior control and responsibility to varying degrees.[152] Cognitive impairment in dissociative disorders can be a mitigating factor in assessing moral and criminal responsibility. But if these disorders leave some cognitive functions associated with planning and decision-making intact, then they would not be an excusing factor.

Dissociation has implications for the role of consciousness in free will. This is practically equivalent to the cognitive, affective, volitional and motor capacity to form and execute action plans in certain bodily movements. It is largely but not entirely a conscious process. Because the motor component of this process is unconscious, an agent need not be fully aware of their movements to control them and have some degree of free will in acting.[153] Indeed, obsessive-compulsive disorder suggests that being overly conscious of one's movements can impair the ability to perform them voluntarily.[154] Moreover, a patient with ideomotor apraxia can perform certain motor tasks without thinking about them but cannot perform them when instructed to do so because of impaired semantic memory. These examples show the importance of unconscious motor functions in effective agency.

## 7 Consciousness and Determining Death

According to the Uniform Determination of Death Act (UDDA) adopted in 1981 and endorsed by the American Academy of Neurology, death occurs when (1) there is irreversible cessation of circulatory and respiratory functions, or (2) irreversible cessation of all brain functions, including the brainstem.[155] These criteria are complementary since irreversible cessation of circulation will result in irreversible cessation of perfusion to the brain. These criteria are consistent with the UK definition of death as irreversible cessation of all brainstem functions.[156] James Bernat argues that "permanent and irreversible cessation of functions are distinct phenomena but are related causally. All functions that are irreversibly lost are also permanently lost (but not vice versa)."[157] Permanent cessation of function is practically equivalent to irreversible cessation when cardiopulmonary resuscitation will not be performed. A more refined definition of the whole-brain criterion is that death occurs when there is permanent cessation of all integrated brain functions.[158]

The UDDA has been the standard medical and legal model for determining when death occurs. It is not a federal statute but a model state statute of death. In 1981, the US President's Commission and the US Uniform Law Commission recommended that the UDDA be adopted by all states. In this same year, the Law Reform Commission of Canada proposed a model statute of death. Unlike the United States, however, it was not enacted in any Canadian province. Some neurologists, anesthesiologists, philosophers, and ethicists have pointed out inconsistences and incoherence in defining death by neurological criteria. These critiques of the UDDA are now being addressed for the first time in forty years.[159]

Some critics of this statute reject the whole-brain criterion and argue that individuals declared brain-dead are not necessarily dead but can remain biologically alive.[160] One example is the recent experiment in which a kidney transplanted from a pig to a brain-dead patient began to function immediately after the procedure.[161] A broader biological definition is that a human being dies when there is permanent cessation of all integrated functions of the body.[162] Alan Shewmon proposed and defended an earlier version of a biological definition of death. He cited cases in which integrated somatic processes in the body continued after all brain functions had ceased. Shewmon described a child with no brainstem function whose body "has grown, overcome infection, and healed wounds."[163] His somatic integration definition shows that different systems of a human organism can continue to function without a functioning brainstem.[164] According to this definition, death occurs when all cellular and metabolic functions in the body permanently cease.

In contrast to these neurobiological and biological definitions, a higher-brain definition of death is that we die when there is permanent loss of integrated cortical functions.[165] As discussed earlier, connections between the upper brain stem, thalamus, and cortex mediate awareness. But awareness may diminish or be lost from cessation of integrated cortical function alone.[166] This is a biopsychological definition because it defines death as the permanent loss of neural functions necessary to generate and sustain the capacity for consciousness. If persons are defined essentially in terms of the capacity for consciousness, then they die when they permanently lose this capacity and the integrated cortical function that generates and sustains it.[167] They die even if integrated brainstem and subcortical functions continue.

Whole-brain and whole-body definitions of death imply that we are essentially biological beings and only nonessentially conscious beings.[168] We have the capacity for consciousness through only one phase of our lives. We begin to exist before the emergence of consciousness and can continue to exist after we permanently lose it. We cease to exist when all brain or bodily functions permanently cease. According to the higher-brain definition, we are essentially biological and psychological (biopsychological) beings who begin to exist when the integrated function of cortical neural networks generates the capacity for consciousness. We cease to exist when this function permanently ceases, and we permanently lose this capacity. Patients in a prolonged but not irreversible coma, or those in a persistent but not permanent VS, have not died because they have not permanently lost the capacity for consciousness. What makes this model medically and ethically controversial is that it implies that irreversibly comatose and permanently vegetative patients have died, contrary to the UDDA. It is controversial because it may permit discontinuing life-sustaining interventions, or initiating life-ending interventions, that would be prohibited by other definitions of death.

These definitions have different implications for when neurologically compromised patients in conscious and unconscious states can benefit from or be harmed by different actions. Ronald Dworkin distinguishes experiential from critical interests.[169] Experiential interests are interests in having pleasurable experiences and avoiding painful ones. They are time-sensitive and refer to a person's immediate sensory responses to stimuli. These interests are satisfied or thwarted in having or avoiding these experiences. They are not the sort of interests that make our lives good or bad on the whole. Critical interests are time-neutral interests the satisfaction or defeat of which makes one's life better or worse overall. "They represent critical judgments rather than just experiential preferences."[170] Critical interests are based on our beliefs and values about how our lives should go and how others should act or refrain from acting in ways that positively or negatively affect us.

Biological functions in general and subcortical functions in particular do not generate or sustain an experiential interest in avoiding pain and suffering or a critical interest in the trajectory of one's life. Whole-brain and somatic conceptions of human life and death cannot account for these interests because the capacity for consciousness is not a necessary condition of these conceptions. Experiential and critical interests are part of a biological and psychological framework that gives meaning to one's life. If the capacity for consciousness is necessary to have experiential interests, and having these interests is necessary to directly benefit from or be harmed by actions or events that realize or thwart them, then individuals cannot be experientially harmed after they permanently lose consciousness. Depending on the level of awareness, a patient with a traumatic or anoxic brain injury may feel pain. The experiential interest in avoiding pain can be satisfied in many cases by administering analgesia. Suffering may not always be relieved by analgesia because a patient may experience it in the absence of pain. One could have both an experiential and a critical interest in avoiding suffering because of its immediate adverse effect on the psyche and more general adverse effect on one's well-being.

A patient with severe cognitive impairment from a traumatic or anoxic brain injury may not have the level of consciousness necessary to sustain a critical interest in the treatment they should receive. But they would have an experiential interest in avoiding pain and suffering from their condition. If they had a critical interest in initiating, foregoing, continuing, or discontinuing life-sustaining treatment and they expressed it in an advance directive, then they could be adversely affected if physicians and families failed to respect it and acted against what the patient would have wanted. The moral force of the critical interest would extend over the patient's psychological and biological life as a whole. They could be adversely affected by others violating this interest when they were permanently unconscious but still biologically alive. While a person must be conscious to develop critical interests, they need not be conscious to benefit from or be harmed by others respecting or failing to respect these interests.

For those who expressed a critical interest in remaining alive until all brain functions had permanently ceased, continuing ANH and other life-sustaining interventions would benefit them by satisfying this interest. Discontinuing these interventions and allowing them to die would harm them by defeating the interest. For those who expressed a critical interest in not remaining alive in a severely compromised neurological state, continuing ANH or other life-sustaining treatment could harm them by failing to respect and defeating this previously expressed interest.

These issues are complicated by the fact that many patients receiving life-sustaining care do not have the level of awareness and cognitive capacity to make decisions about this care. At some point before the brain injury, they may have changed their mind about the sorts of interventions they would want, or want to avoid, after expressing a different wish earlier in conversation or an advance directive. When patients are unconscious or in a diminished conscious state, families can make substitute decisions for them. But their decisions may not always accurately reflect the patient's wishes at particular times or over time. Equally significant, patients could not change their minds and have different attitudes about care once they had lost consciousness. Some who retained a certain level of awareness and cognition in an MCS might have the mental capacity to change their critical interests and wishes about treatments that were consistent with them.

As discussed in Section 5.3, behaviorally nonresponsive patients with the requisite cognitive and motor capacities could use a BCI to clearly and reliably express wishes and decisions about medical care. But this technology would not help those who were permanently unconscious. In these cases, the default position would be to uphold the moral and legal force of the wishes expressed in an advance directive. For those without a directive or families to make substitute decisions for them, the default position would be to continue care until all brain and circulatory functions permanently ceased. This could benefit those who would have wanted to continue living but harm those who would not have wanted it.

Conceptions and definitions of death that conflict with the UDDA can present challenges to physicians and courts regarding treatment of patients in critical care. In most cases, physicians will declare death based on permanent loss of integrated whole-brain and circulatory function. Families making substitute decisions for noncompetent patients may agree with this determination. But the case of Jahi McMath is a noteworthy exception to these practices.

Three teams of neurologists determined that Jahi was brain-dead following complications from an adenotonsillectomy in December 2013. The blood loss caused brain anoxia leading to the permanent loss of all brain functions. Her mother, Nailah Winkfield, made two distinct legal claims in arguing that Jahi was not dead.[171] First, she claimed that her daughter's brain function was not irreversibly lost. Second, she claimed that, even if Jahi had no brain function, she was not dead as long as her circulation and respiration continued. This apparently ignored the fact that these functions continued because of artificial ventilatory support. The second legal claim noted evidence of sexual maturation and menstruation, which could only occur with an active hypothalamus. Consistent with the somatic integration definition of life and death, hormonal secretions and other bodily processes may continue for some time without a functioning brain. For Winkfield, Jahi continued to live despite the fact that she had permanently lost brain functions necessary to sustain the capacity for consciousness. Indeed, she continued to live despite the loss of all integrated brain functions. Winkfield's second claim suggested that her daughter was essentially a biological organism who was conscious only through the phase of her life before the surgery.

The McMath case is in stark contrast to the earlier case of Nancy Cruzan. She sustained a severe brain injury in an automobile accident in 1983, becoming comatose and progressing to a persistent and then permanent VS. She was kept alive by ANH. Her parents claimed that she should be allowed to die and sought a court order to remove the feeding tube. But this was overruled by the Missouri Supreme Court. The Court claimed that there was no clear and convincing evidence of Nancy's desire to have life-sustaining treatment withheld or withdrawn under the circumstances. In 1990, the US Supreme Court upheld the right of the state of Missouri to require strict standards of evidence regarding the patient's preferences. Yet the Court also affirmed the fundamental principle of a patient's right to forgo life-sustaining treatment and supported the parents' decision by ordering the discontinuation of ANH in 1990.[172] This was seven years after Nancy had progressed from a coma to a permanent VS.

The parents' substitute decision was based on their belief that Nancy would not have wanted life-sustaining treatment if she became permanently unconscious and completely dependent on others. Although she could not express her wishes, her presumed earlier wish not to remain alive in a VS was a critical interest that applied to all the stages of her life, including the last stage. Keeping her alive defeated this interest and was a form of nonexperiential harm. Her parents engraved the following inscription on Nancy's gravestone: "Departed Jan.11, 1983/At Peace Dec. 26, 1990."[173] It is not clear what they actually believed about when she died. But the first part of this inscription suggests that she died when she permanently lost the capacity for consciousness after her brain injury. This involved permanent cessation of all integrated cortical functions before permanent cessation of all integrated subcortical and brainstem functions. It occurred before she was declared biologically dead after the feeding tube was removed.

The UDDA provides the standard medical and legal definition of death. Yet Jahi McMath's mother appeared to believe in a biological definition of life and death not requiring continued natural brain function. Nancy Cruzan's family appeared to believe in a higher-brain definition. This definition implies that the capacity for consciousness is what makes one a person with a critical interest in how one's life should go. They believed that whether a person benefits from or is harmed by life-sustaining treatment depends on their capacity for awareness and the brain regions that support it. Only conscious individuals can develop critical interests. But the situations in which these interests are realized or defeated may obtain after they have lost consciousness. While most families' beliefs align with the UDDA and the whole-brain/circulatory criterion of death, the two cases that I have presented illustrate that there is no universally accepted definition of death among the general public.

The fraught debate on when death occurs suggests that it is not just a biological fact but also a social and cultural one. Beliefs about the sorts of beings we are influence how we define death. Since these beliefs vary across people, there is no single monolithic definition of what death is or when we die. Robert Veatch and Lainie Friedman Ross argue that "choosing a definition of death for public policy and other social purposes is, in fact, a philosophical, religious, or social choice. ... We are, in effect, trying to identify the moment at which society should decide that someone is no longer with us and that we should treat that person the way we treat the dead."[174] They add that "We should give people some space to make personal, conscientious choices among plausible definitions [of death]."[175] Veatch and Friedman Ross claim that allowing for choice in defining death would not lead to policy chaos if policy decisions were tolerant of variation in religious and philosophical beliefs.[176] Within a certain degree of reasonableness, physicians, medical institutions, and the courts can be sensitive to and accommodate these differences in allowing some discretion among individuals and families choosing which conception of death to adopt.

Still, the higher-brain criterion is necessary to ground experiential and critical interests. It is the most plausible conception to ground and frame ethical questions about continuing or discontinuing life-sustaining care. Integrated cortical function is necessary to generate and sustain the capacity for consciousness necessary to have an interest in whether one's life should continue or end. No matter how integrated its functions may be, a biological organism without the capacity for consciousness cannot have an interest in how actions or events affect it. Biological or neurobiological processes alone do not generate interests. These are products of mental life that emerges from the activity of distributed neural networks, specifically cortical networks, when they reach a certain level of complexity. Nancy Cruzan's parents relied at least implicitly on this conception in arguing that life-sustaining treatment should have been withdrawn from their daughter. When a patient has a brain injury resulting in the permanent loss of the capacity for consciousness, they have ceased to exist. This can be confirmed by structural and functional neuroimaging showing diffuse axonal injury and widespread damage to gray and white matter tracts in cortical and subcortical regions.

This judgment reflects the belief that persons are essentially biological and psychological beings defined in terms of the neurobiological and psychological properties associated with consciousness. A human organism can remain alive with a certain level of integrated bodily function.[177] This may include subcortical and brain stem activity. But if personhood consists essentially in the capacity for consciousness, then a person ceases to exist when the integrated function of the cortical networks supporting this capacity permanently ceases.

Critical and experiential interests are not biological features but features of a person's conscious mental states. These states depend on but are not reducible to connections between the upper brainstem and thalamus, the thalamus and cortex, and different cortical regions. Questions about the moral permissibility or impermissibility of initiating, withholding, continuing or discontinuing life-support hinge on whether these actions benefit or harm patients, and these depend on whether they have interests and the capacity for consciousness that underlies them. A critical interest can obligate others to perform or refrain from performing actions affecting patients' bodies when they have only minimal or no consciousness. They can benefit from or be harmed by these actions even though they cannot experience their effects because the content of the interest may extend to the end of and even beyond their biological lives.

## 7.1 Unconsciousness and Organ Donation

It is instructive to apply these considerations to organ donation. Would it be morally permissible to procure organs viable for transplantation from patients who are permanently unconscious, or minimally conscious, but not imminently dying? As in the preceding section, the core ethical question is not when a person is declared dead by whole-brain or somatic integration criteria, but whether they retain the capacity for awareness and have interests in what happens to them. Depending on whether they have consented to organ donation, this determines whether they can benefit from or be harmed by removing organs from their bodies. Only a biopsychological model indicating when a person has or loses the capacity for consciousness can answer these questions. They pertain not to *brains* and *bodies* but to *persons* who are constituted by but not identical to them.[178]

The dead donor rule (DDR) is an extension and practical application of the UDDA. As the ethical and legal foundation of deceased organ donation, the DDR states that donors must be declared dead before vital organs can be procured from their bodies for the purpose of transplantation. Death is pronounced according to whole-brain or circulatory criteria. The DDR protects critical care and transplant teams from criminal liability. It also promotes confidence in the transplant system by reassuring the public that under no circumstances (even with donor consent) will vital organs be procured from living people. It prevents donors from being killed for the sake of their organs.

Some physicians and ethicists have questioned the DDR and proposed an alternative model of deceased organ donation based on patient autonomy and nonmaleficence. It is not the time when death is declared that matters morally in this type of organ donation but whether the patient consents to donation and is protected from harm. The DDR implies that a patient would be harmed if organs were procured before a declaration of death. Referring to circulatory death, David Rodriguez-Arias, Maxwell Smith, and Neil Lazar ask: "Under which conditions would it be morally acceptable to procure vital organs from dying patients"? They respond: "Ultimately, what is important for the protection and respect of potential donors is not to have a death certificate signed, but rather to be certain that they are beyond suffering and to guarantee that their autonomy is respected. The DDR hardly serves these morally necessary purposes. Rather, it might be pulling our attention from them."[179] They raise an additional question: "If donors are beyond harm and had given appropriate consent for donation, would it really be necessary to call them dead?"[180]

Would a patient with a severe brain injury be harmed if they had consented to organ donation, and organs viable for transplantation were taken from their body when they were permanently unconscious but still neurologically and biologically alive? Patients who were irreversibly comatose or permanently vegetative but not imminently dying would not be experientially harmed because they had permanently lost the capacity for consciousness. Could they be harmed in other respects?

Many people have a critical interest in continuing to live, even with serious chronic illness. They can be harmed by death because it defeats this critical interest. For those with a critical interest in living independently until a natural demise, life-sustaining treatment such as ventilation or ANH can harm them by defeating this interest. We may also have critical interests in states of affairs that extend beyond the capacity for awareness. These interests can survive the death of a person who had them, regardless of whether one accepts a higher-brain, whole-brain, or somatic integration definition of death. They may include an interest in having one's organs transplanted after one has died. This may appear to be consistent with the DDR. But it would not be consistent with it if one believes that one dies when one permanently loses the capacity for consciousness.

Individuals who intend to donate cannot benefit experientially but can benefit nonexperientially after death if their organs are successfully transplanted and their intention is realized. They can be harmed nonexperientially if their organs are viable, but family members violate first-person authorization of a consenting individual by prohibiting organ procurement for transplantation.[181] This would violate the donor's precedent autonomy expressed in their wish to donate. Individuals intending to donate could also be harmed if critical care and transplant teams waited until death was declared by the whole-brain definition, by which time organs could be ischemic and not viable for transplantation. Those who uphold this definition could claim that withdrawing life-support and initiating organ procurement before permanent cessation of all integrated brain functions would be killing the patient. But if one accepts the higher-brain definition of death, then a permanently unconscious patient who previously expressed an interest in donating their organs could benefit and not be harmed if organs were procured before the permanent loss of these functions. The patient would have died before these functions ceased.

Franklin Miller, Robert Truog, and Dan Brock generally agree with Rodriguez-Arias, Smith, and Lazar in rejecting the DDR.[182] They also argue that "organ donation should be permissible from those who are imminently dying or permanently unconscious."[183] It is important to distinguish different groups of neurologically compromised patients and whether or at what level they are conscious. Assuming that being conscious implies being aware and not just awake, those who are permanently unconscious and unaware include patients in an irreversible coma or a permanent VS. They are distinct from patients in a MCS with some degree of awareness. These patients in turn are distinct from those with ALS or LIS, who are fully conscious but have severe motor limitations and extensive paralysis. The time from diagnosis to death in ALS and LIS is variable and can range from approximately two to ten years. They are not strictly speaking imminently dying. But they may have a critical interest in donating their organs for transplantation and may have retained the cognitive capacity to consent to donation. Depending on the condition of their organs, procurement may occur before a declaration of death to prevent ischemia and other factors that could adversely affect their viability for transplantation. Analgesia or sedation could be administered to prevent or mitigate any pain they may feel during procurement. While this violates the UDDA and DDR, in principle it could be justified if an ALS or LIS patient consented to donation and understood what the timing of procurement would mean for their demise.

The disjunction "or" in the passage from Miller, Truog, and Brock suggests that the imminently dying and the permanently unconscious are distinct groups defined by distinct diagnostic criteria. A patient in a permanent VS or irreversible coma is permanently unconscious. The morally relevant aspect of consciousness is not arousal but awareness, since this state is what allows a patient to feel pain, suffer, or have a critical interest in how their life should go. But they may not be imminently dying, and some patients can live for years in either of these states. For permanently comatose or vegetative patients who consented to organ donation and indicated before their brain injury that they would not want to continue living in these states, procuring their organs before a declaration of death could be permissible despite the fact that it did not follow but resulted in their death.

Patients with impaired consciousness, such as those in the MCS, may have expressed a preference for or against organ donation before their brain injury. For those who maintain a certain level of cognitive function, they may change their mind about donation after the injury but not be able to communicate it. This could affect them differently depending on their critical interests. For those who did not want to donate, leaving organs in their bodies after a declaration of death would realize their interest. For those who wanted to donate, not procuring and transplanting their organs would defeat their interest. This could occur if organs were not viable from failure to remove life-support and initiate procurement before a declaration of death. Organ procurement is typically based on a competent patient's current preferences about organ donation. The inability to communicate these preferences can affect patients positively or negatively. These considerations assume that peoples' critical interests can persist through impaired consciousness and can survive after they have permanently lost consciousness.

Organ procurement occurring before a declaration of death according to whole-brain or circulatory criteria could be described as a form of organ donation euthanasia (ODE). Dominic Wilkinson and Julian Savulescu ask:

> Why should surgeons have to wait until the patient has died as a result of withdrawal of advanced life-support or even simple life-prolonging medical treatment? An alternative would be to anaesthetize the patient and remove organs, including the heart and lungs. Brain death would follow removal of the heart .... If there were a careful and appropriate process for selection, no patient would die who would not otherwise have died.[184]

The last sentence of this passage implies that only patients who are imminently dying would be appropriate candidates for ODE. But many permanently unconscious patients are not imminently dying and can remain unconscious for an extended period. These include those in prolonged comas and those in the permanent VS. If they lacked awareness and could not feel pain or suffer, then they would be beyond any experiential harm. One could make this claim even if these patients would have continued living but for this action. They could only be harmed nonexperientially by ODE if they objected to organ donation, did not consent to it, and rejected opt-out policies allowing procurement without consent. In that case, ODE would harm them by defeating their critical interest in what happens to their body, regardless of their neurological status.

Although organ procurement has been initiated before a declaration of death in some cases of consenting ALS patients,[185] many if not most critical care and transplant teams would not do this because it would violate the UDDA and DDR. Presumably, it would also violate their obligation of nonmaleficence not to harm patients by causing their death. But unless the patient wanted to continue living, death would not harm them in any experiential sense. They could benefit nonexperientially from procurement and transplantation if the content of their interest in organ donation extended beyond their death. They could be harmed nonexperientially if this interest were defeated by not transplanting their organs because of ischemia, a family override of the patient's consent, or physicians refusing to procure them before a declaration of whole-brain or circulatory death. What matters morally in organ procurement for transplantation is not whether a consenting patient has been declared dead or is imminently dying. Rather, what matters is their level of awareness, whether they have interests, and whether these interests are realized or defeated by procuring and transplanting their organs. Still, these considerations must be weighed against current procurement policies that promote and maintain public confidence in the transplant system.

## 8 Altering Consciousness near the End of Life

Pain in advanced cancer is often refractory to analgesia. Incremental doses of opioids or sedation can relieve pain and suffering but diminish consciousness. Most patients would prefer pain relief that did not result in the loss of awareness of self and surroundings. This precludes interaction with families and others that gives value to the last hours, days, and weeks of their lives. Alternatives to analgesia may avoid this situation and relieve pain by altering a patient's perception and other cognitive and affective aspects of their experience. These include meditation, hypnosis, and psychotropic or hallucinogenic drugs such as ketamine and psilocybin that can dissociate a patient from their body and alter their perception of time. In these two respects, these interventions can alleviate pain and suffering in dying. However, their efficacy depends on a patient's cognitive and affective capacity to respond to them. This capacity is absent in delirium, a disturbed state of consciousness characterized by confused thinking, anxiety, hallucinations, and reduced awareness of the environment.[186]

Delirium can result from infection, metabolic imbalance, advanced cancer, prolonged hospitalization, or other factors that disturb neurotransmitter and other neural functions mediating psychomotor and cognitive processing. While delirium may resolve by treating infections and restoring metabolic balance, it may be irreversible in terminal disease. In these cases, the disorder progresses from disturbed consciousness to unconsciousness and then death. Patients are beyond hope of any meaningful social interaction.

In addition to its immediate aversive sensory experience, intractable pain can cause suffering by causing a patient to expect its continuation. In end-stage cancer and other diseases, suffering can be exacerbated by fearful anticipation of continued pain and death. This is why so many terminally ill patients experience anxiety and depression. For those without prolonged delirium, different interventions may ease the experience of dying by altering consciousness.

Meditation can make one less attentive to the body as the source of pain and more attentive to other aspects of their awareness. This may include a focus on one's breathing and temporary suspension or reduction of other sensory experience.[187] Virtual reality programs can also manage pain by altering the content of consciousness. Yet the efficacy of this treatment modality, as well as meditation, requires attention and patience that many people in severe pain may not have or be able to sustain. Hypnosis may be a more effective alternative.

"Hypnosis uses the powerful effects of attention and suggestion to produce, modify and enhance a broad range of subjectively compelling experiences and behaviors."[188] The goal of this technique is to enable the patient to modulate autonomic processes underlying chronic pain, addiction, and other conditions. Hypnosis typically involves inducing a series of suggestions for the participant to adopt. These suggestions enable them to become more focused and absorbed in a particular mental state. Participants tend to be "less distracted by outside stimuli and less likely to engage in analytical thinking with their minds being less crowded with thoughts and associations."[189] Functional imaging studies of patients undergoing hypnosis have shown reduced activity in their default mode network, or normal resting state, and increased activity in prefrontal attention and executive systems.[190] Hypnosis can also reduce activity in subcortical regions mediating fear, as well as the insular cortex, which mediates the subjective experience of duration and moving through time.[191] In addition, hypnosis can modulate "activity in the neural pain matrix" and in turn "modulate sensory and affective (emotional) components of . . . pain experience."[192] Some have questioned whether a hypnotic trance should be described as a "unique state of consciousness"[193] or an altered state of consciousness. If hypnosis involves explicit recognition that one's subjective experience has changed, then it would be appropriate to describe it as an altered conscious state.

Although a person is unaware of some of the cognitive processes involved in hypnosis, some conscious cognitive and affective capacities are necessary for the participant to respond to the suggestions. In contrast to meditation, the unconscious aspects of suggestion can make hypnosis less cognitively and emotionally demanding for the participant and more effective in alleviating pain and suffering. This may allow the patient to feel that they have some psychological control over the somatic effects of a biologically uncontrolled disease. A critical component of this control and ethical justification for hypnosis for a dying patient is their informed consent to participate in it. This presupposes that the disease has not impaired their capacity for reasoning and decision-making about psychological, behavioral, or pharmacological interventions. It also presupposes that pain and fear networks in the brain can be downregulated by the patient's response to the suggestions.

Eric Cassell describes the case of a patient with stomach cancer for whom hypnosis alleviated suffering associated with treatment by altering her temporal awareness. After completing a course of chemotherapy, she would fearfully anticipate the next course. Hypnosis altered her perception of duration. This significantly reduced her anticipation of the next round of chemotherapy and mitigated her fear and anxiety about it. The treatments "are not there until they suddenly 'arrive,' and then they quickly disappear. Although weakness, some nausea, and poor appetite lasted for a brief period post chemotherapy, the problem had greatly lessened, as had the anticipation of the next treatment."[194]

Antonio Damasio and coinvestigators have reported similar effects of hypnosis. In experiments designed to manage chronic intractable pain, hypnotic suggestions were given to a group of patients. The suggestions reduced their perception of pain and emotional reaction to it. PET scans showed that hypnosis altered their perception by causing changes in the primary somatosensory cortex and cingulate cortex.[195] Hypnosis may be most beneficial to patients with intense pain and fear of dying in the last stage of their life by altering different aspects of their awareness. Like meditation, though, its efficacy depends on certain cognitive and emotional capacities that many of these patients either lack or cannot sustain.

Just before his death, Tolstoy's Ivan Ilych dissociates himself from his cancer-ridden body to overcome pain. He also alters his perception of time to overcome his fear of death. He does this without any external aids but with his own psychological resources. While Ivan is a fictional character, actual people can have a similar experience just before death. These cases may be relatively rare and influenced by one's religious beliefs. But it is instructive to review

Tolstoy's description of the last moments of Ivan's life and a recent commentary on it to show how a change in the content of consciousness can positively affect a person's experience of dying.

After a life of purely self-interested ambition, Ivan displays empathy and sympathy for those around him in the last moments of his life. By shifting his focus from himself to others, he alters his perception of pain and time. "Yes, there it is. Well, let there be pain. And death? Where is it?" "He sought his old habitual fear of death and could not find it. There was no more fear because there was no more death."[196] "For him, all this happened in an instant and the significance of that instant never changed."[197] The feeling of suspended temporal duration allows Ivan to experience a sense of timelessness that dissolves his anticipation of pain and fear of death. If the passage of time has ceased, then he cannot progress to death and cannot die. The meaning of Tolstoy's description of Ivan's epiphany is captured in Wittgenstein's later comment: "Death is not an event in life: we do not live to experience death. If we take eternity to mean not infinite temporal duration but timelessness, then eternal life belongs to those who live in the present."[198]

Frances Kamm offers an insightful interpretation of the cited passages from Tolstoy's novella:

> Because Ivan comes to live so completely in the moment, he may think that there is no death. For if our *sense* of time moving on (to death) is a function of felt changes taking place, then constancy gives rise to the sense that time is not passing and that this moment will never end. Hence, looked at secularly, Ivan may say that there is no death because he is so engrossed in the experience of his new insight and new nature that he is subject to a new illusion, namely that he in his new state will not die."[199]

There is another sense in which Ivan transcends pain and death by transcending the fearful anticipation associated with them. His identification with those around him and his living through them may be so complete that "he" has ceased to exist.[200] Ivan's awareness of himself as a persisting subject has substantially changed. In the conclusion to his argument against the idea of persons as persisting beings and the impossibility of his own death, Mark Johnston claims that "all room for the thought of my *ownmost death* – the end of this very arena of presence and action – has disappeared."[201] Ivan overcomes pain, fear, and death through a dissolution of his self.

Most patients experiencing pain and suffering at the end of life lack the psychological resources of Ivan Ilych to mitigate or transcend them. If they are not candidates for hypnosis, then anesthetics like ketamine and psychedelics like psilocybin and 3,4 methylenedioxymethamphetamine (MDMA) can alter consciousness. The purpose of using these drugs for these patients is not to dissolve the self or generate an illusion of timeless eternity as ends in themselves. Instead, the purpose is to mitigate distress from pain and fear of dying caused by consciously feeling and anticipating them. The drugs produce these therapeutic effects by causing patients to feel dissociated from their body and modifying their sense of time.

Studies testing the effects of these drugs have been designed primarily to ease end-of-life anxiety and depression in patients terminally ill with stage-4 cancers. These are not symptoms of chronic mental illness but an adverse response to disease. A pilot study involving twelve subjects completed in 2008 and published in 2011 showed that administering psychedelics in a controlled setting with selective patients and careful dosing was safe and effective in achieving these therapeutic goals.[202] Although this treatment is still experimental, it can be one component of palliative care. Treatment sessions typically last from five to seven hours. Patients are given black eyeshades and headphones with music piped in as the drugs are infused intravenously. Among other neural factors, anxiety has been associated with a hyperactive anterior cingulate cortex (ACC). Psilocybin can downregulate this activity and relieve symptoms in patients with generalized anxiety disorder. It can also relieve this symptom in patients with advanced cancer. Ketamine can cause a feeling of dissociation between the subject and their body through its effects on the neurotransmitter glutamate in the ACC and adjacent brain regions.[203] The use of these drugs by healthy individuals in uncontrolled settings may have deleterious effects by disrupting perception and impairing decision-making and effective agency. But they can have salutary effects for patients with terminal disease when complemented with psychological support.

A later double-blind, placebo-controlled crossover trial tested the effects of psilocybin on anxiety and depression in twenty-nine patients with advanced breast, gastrointestinal, and blood cancers.[204] Many of the patients reported rapid and sustained symptom relief. As in the 2011 study described previously, the control drug in this study was niacin, which has no significant effect on the content of mental states. This leaves open the possibility that the altered conscious states were a placebo response rather than a neurophysiological effect of psilocybin. But it is unlikely that a person would experience such alterations of consciousness from a placebo.

A more recent study involving nineteen patients with major depressive disorder showed increased resting-state blood flow measured by fMRI following administration of psilocybin. The fact that half of the patients had symptom improvement that continued for up to five weeks after one treatment suggests that the altered conscious states associated with the drug are more than a placebo effect.[205] There is an ongoing debate about weighing the therapeutic effects of ego-dissolution with psilocybin in combination with psychotherapy and the potential deleterious effects I have mentioned.[206] Although patients with chronic depression are different from patients with acute depression in response to disease and imminent death, the neural and mental effects of psilocybin are similar in both groups.

Some patients in these studies report an absence of fear and a feeling of calm or peace in accepting death. Other patients report feeling altruistic. Still others report feeling dissociated from their bodies and experiencing a dissolution of the self into the world with no perceived boundary between them. In addition to their downregulating effects on the ACC, psychedelics can alter activity in the insular cortex regulating one's perception of space and time, and somatosensory cortex regulating proprioception (perception of body position and self-movement), interoception (perception of the internal state of the body), and exteroception (perception of objects in the external world).[207] These drugs can cause these changes more rapidly and dramatically than hypnosis because of their more direct effects on these brain regions. Some patients receiving psilocybin report having transformative spiritual experiences. The perceived dissociation of the patient from their body and the temporary disruption of the experience of duration can reduce pain, anxiety, and suffering by disrupting the neural networks mediating these experiences.

The dissolution of self that some patients experience psychologically from the drug's effects on the brain can reduce or even eliminate the fear of death. It is similar in some respects to the reported ego-dissolution in patients with near-death experiences.[208] Like Ivan Ilych, if there is no self, then "it" cannot die. The effect of abolishing the thought of death from the patient with these drugs is temporary and not immune to bodily decline and the demise of the organism. But psychedelics can ameliorate a patient's psychological response to disease and imminent death.[209]

These are salutary aspects of drug-induced temporary alteration of different aspects of awareness. Assuming that selective patients give informed consent to this treatment, that it is administered in a controlled setting with careful dosing, and that there is no risk of self-harm during or after treatment sessions, psilocybin, ketamine, and MDMA can be medically and ethically justified as forms of palliative care. Even if there were some neurological and psychological sequelae from these treatments, the benefit of alleviating pain, suffering, and the fear of death could outweigh the harm from these sequelae in the last stage of a patient's life. The fact that death is imminent and that the goal is palliation in these cases distinguishes them from psychedelic psychiatry for chronic disorders such as major depression and anxiety. Although a physician's infusion of a drug to alter consciousness might suggest loss of control of the patient's thought and behavior, patients have some control of the process when they deliberatively consent to and voluntarily receive a treatment that can calm the psyche and ease distress in the face of death.

## 8.1 Suppressing and Restoring Consciousness

In many patients with advanced cancer and other terminal diseases, high-dose opioids or sedation may be the only way to keep them comfortable. These pharmacological interventions can diminish awareness or cause unconsciousness. Continuous deep sedation suppressing consciousness can gradually result in the patient's death. The mechanism through which it causes or accelerates death is usually dehydration because the patient cannot drink when deeply sedated. Also, intravenous fluid administration is often limited to medications. Whether the goal of sedation is to relieve suffering or deliberately induce unconsciousness until death has been an ethically controversial issue for decades, and I will return to it shortly. Here I consider some of the trade-offs between the benefit of suppressing a patient's consciousness to prevent pain and the benefit of not suppressing it to allow the patient to meaningfully interact with others near the end of their life. Suppressing consciousness can benefit a patient by eliminating pain. But it can harm them by precluding this interaction. Not all patients react to pain in the same way. Some may not be able to tolerate pain, and drug-induced unconsciousness may be the only way to treat it.

Whether pain and suffering are tolerable depends not only on how the patient responds physiologically but also psychologically to them and their immediate environment. Some patients would welcome unconsciousness as a release from a life that had lost meaning and value for them. Others would want to remain conscious and retain their mental faculties and connection to the outside world for as long as possible. This may include not only patients who are surrounded by loved ones but also those who die alone. Continued life would have value for them, even if they were in pain. Freud refused to take anything stronger than aspirin until the end of his painful ordeal with terminal oral cancer. Concerned that opiates would cloud his consciousness, he reportedly said: "I prefer to think in torment than not to be able to think at all."[210] These judgments about the value or disvalue of consciousness at the end of life depend on the unique experiential and critical interests of each patient.

In a less common scenario, discontinuing or reducing the dosage of a sedative could allow an unconscious patient or one with diminished consciousness to regain enough awareness to interact with physicians and families. This assumes that the disease was not so far advanced that restoration of consciousness would be physiologically impossible. Less severe diminished awareness is not salutary if it involves confusion and distress, as in delirium. Unconsciousness may be preferable to any degree of awareness allowing these negative experiences.

The question of whether to restore consciousness in these cases may generate as much uncertainty between physicians and families as the question of whether to induce diminished consciousness or unconsciousness to control or eliminate pain. The value of social interaction from restored consciousness must be weighed against the disvalue of restoring the ability to feel pain and suffer. Different patients may weigh these states differently from a baseline conscious state. One can only hypothesize about a patient's wishes based on comments they may have made before sedative- or opioid-induced unconsciousness. In consultation with physicians, families could make substitute decisions about whether or to what extent to increase or reduce sedation or opioids in the patient. When consciousness can be restored, there may not be a solid basis for a decision to reduce or discontinue sedation because it is unlikely that this would have been discussed while the patient was conscious. It is not a request that would be included in a typical advance directive.

Family members could give proxy consent to discontinue sedation to allow them to interact with the patient. This scenario could arise when a family member was not available to discuss treatment options for a patient until after they had been sedated. There would be uncertainty about whether the positive aspects of restoring a patient's awareness in order to interact with them would outweigh the negative aspects of being aware. This may not be known until after awareness had been restored. Not all patients would want this. For some, though, the value of having last words with loved ones could outweigh the disvalue of experiencing pain. This type of meaningful interaction could shift the patient's focus away from the symptoms of their disease. Discontinuing opioids or sedation to allow this interaction would be based on the relationship between the patient and family or caregivers before they lost consciousness.

In some cases, a request by a family member to temporarily reduce or discontinue sedation, restore consciousness, and enable communication may be motivated more by a desire to relieve guilt about a failed emotional relationship with the patient than by respecting their wish for last words. This could benefit the family member but harm the patient if they had no critical interest in it. Restoring consciousness to enable interaction could be ethically justified only if there was evidence of a positive emotional relationship between them and if comments by the patient before losing consciousness indicated that this is what they would have wanted.

The significance of retaining or regaining consciousness in order to interact with others near or at the end of life is one example of Frith's and Zeman's points about the social aspect of consciousness. It enables a person not just to be aware of but also to relate to and engage with the social environment. Depending on their duration, the dissociative effects of psychedelics can interfere with or preclude this interaction. This is one consideration against using these agents in terminally ill patients. Psychedelics alter consciousness; opioids and sedation diminish or abolish it. The effects of all these agents can inhibit the patient's ability to respond to others in a meaningful way. A patient in an altered state of consciousness or unconsciousness would not have the cognitive and emotional capacity to weigh the value of interaction against the value of reducing or eliminating pain, anxiety, and depression when they were in the depths of a terminal disease. The ethical justification for altering consciousness with psychedelics, diminishing or suppressing it with opioids or sedation, and retaining or restoring it by foregoing or discontinuing these interventions would depend on the patient's social relations and knowledge of their previously expressed preferences about end-of-life care.

## 8.2 Palliative Sedation and Terminal Anesthesia

Antony Takla, Julian Savulescu, and Dominic Wilkinson discuss the medical and ethical rationale for three types of end-of-life care for patients with treatment-refractory diseases: symptom-based management with analgesia; proportional terminal sedation to relieve suffering; and deliberate and rapid sedation or anesthesia to unconsciousness until death. They also describe the second intervention as "palliative sedation" or "continuous deep sedation," and the third intervention as "terminal anesthesia."[211] Analgesics like morphine, fentanyl, and oxycodone relieve pain but can diminish consciousness as an unintended side effect.[212] Sedation and anesthesia relieve pain and suffering by diminishing or suppressing consciousness. Sedation is "deep" when it causes unconsciousness by disrupting brainstem, subcortical, and cortical networks mediating wakefulness and awareness. In continuous deep sedation to unconsciousness, death is not the goal but a foreseeable side effect of a palliative intervention. In terminal anesthesia, inducing unconsciousness until death is not a side effect but the goal of the intervention.

Terminal anesthesia may be indicated when the patient's suffering cannot be controlled by the common palliative medications. Benzodiazepines and opioids can control agitation, fear, dyspnea, delirium, or psychosis. But these agents are not always effective in controlling these states. Gradually or rapidly inducing unconsciousness and death by sedation or anesthesia may be the only way to relieve suffering.

Questions regarding the ethical justification of the three types of end-of-life care often involve an appeal to the doctrine of double effect (DDE).[213]

According to the DDE, an action with harmful effects is permissible if and only if it meets four criteria:

1. The action itself must be good, independent of its consequences.
2. Although the bad effect is foreseeable, the agent must intend only the good effect.
3. The bad effect must not be a means to the good effect.
4. The good effect must outweigh, or be proportional to, the bad effect.

A hypothetical case to which the DDE can be applied is one in which physicians administer continuous deep sedation to control a terminally ill patient's pain. The effects of the drugs on the patient's respiration and other physiological processes gradually result in their death. The intended good effect of pain control outweighs the foreseeable but unintended bad effect of death, which was not the means to control pain. This action meets all four criteria of the DDE. One shortcoming of the DDE is that it is generally applied to justify actions by physicians. It does not adequately account for the preferences of the competent patient and requests they make that are consistent with these preferences. Ethical justification of an action that diminishes or suppresses consciousness and gradually or rapidly causes death depends not only on the physician's intention but also on the interventions a patient wants to have or avoid in the last stage of their life. The four criteria of the DDE should apply to both the physician and the patient.

In cases where analgesia fails to control pain, sedation may be necessary to control it. Sedation does not always cause unconsciousness. Moderate sedation may keep patients comfortable while maintaining some level of awareness. When pain and suffering are severe, deep sedation or anesthesia may be necessary to suppress the neural and mental processes that allow a patient to experience them. Many physicians and ethicists claim that there is a morally significant distinction between continuous deep sedation and terminal anesthesia. The physician's intention in the first action is palliation. Their intention in the second action is to cause unconsciousness until death. But the fact that the patient's death is the known outcome of both actions seems to blur the boundary between them.

The cognitive and volitional components in intending to induce unconsciousness and the cognitive component in foreseeing the outcome of the action are morally significant because both the action and its outcome are included in the content of the physician's mental states when they act. Insofar as the physician has cognitive control in knowing the likely sequence of events and outcome in administering sedation or anesthesia, the distinction between gradually inducing permanent unconsciousness and rapidly inducing it is not morally significant. If a patient wanted and consented to being rendered permanently unconscious, then whether they died sooner rather than later would not matter morally if both actions achieved the same goal. Either of these actions could benefit the patient by ending their negative experience. There is no moral asymmetry between palliative sedation and terminal sedation because it is not death that harms the patient but continued pain and suffering from being aware.

Some may be skeptical of the presumed reasonableness of wanting to end one's life before a terminal illness runs its course. Yet even if an intentionally caused death is bad, allowing continued pain and suffering is worse. One cannot experience the first because death is not an event in life but the end of experience and the end of life.[214] As Kamm points out, "the intention to die is sometimes reasonable and morally acceptable when death is the less bad option that helps avoid a worse option."[215]

This argument is similar in some respects to the distinction between killing and letting die. It involves the presumed morally significant distinction between intending to cause a patient's death by performing an action and not intending but foreseeing death as a side effect of an action.[216] As in the alleged morally significant distinction between gradually inducing unconsciousness with the goal of palliation and rapidly inducing it with the goal of death, the distinction between killing and letting die is not morally significant when the agent has cognitive control over the sequence of events extending from the action to the outcome. This control consists in knowing what the last event in the sequence will be when they initiate the sequence by infusing the sedative or anesthetic. Here too, the core ethical issues are not just the physician's intention in acting and knowing its outcome but also the patient's interest and whether the action and outcome are consistent with and realize this interest. Unlike Freud, for competent patients voluntarily requesting terminal anesthesia, awareness has no value but only disvalue. Any interest in retaining one's mental faculties and personal interaction is outweighed by an interest in permanently being released from an intolerable dying process.

Daniel Sulmasy argues that consciousness is an objective human good for patients who are dying, as well as for those who are not dying. There is a cost when physicians diminish or suppress it with sedation or anesthesia.[217] Yet one could plausibly claim that the capacity for consciousness does not exist independently of persons; it is an essential property of being a person. Whether it is good or bad is not an objective fact but depends on what the person is conscious of and their subjective experience of it. If there is an objective cost to induced unconsciousness, then it is unclear how it would affect the patient. Sulmasy further argues that proportional, or "parsimonious," sedation to unconsciousness is permissible only in "extremely rare cases in which the patient's consciousness has been completely consumed by symptoms and no less dramatic alternatives are on hand."[218] Parsimonious sedation means using only "as much therapeutic force as necessary" to achieve the desired goal.[219] Directly intending unconsciousness in dying patients with terminal sedation to hasten, or directly cause, death is not parsimonious and therefore impermissible. It fails to meet the third criterion of the DDE. Still, continuous deep sedation to unconsciousness could meet the third and fourth criteria of the DDE if it was necessary to relieve suffering.[220]

The moral justification of parsimonious sedation or terminal anesthesia depends not only on what the physician intends and foresees but also on the patient's wishes. If a patient wanted relief from suffering while continuing to live, and analgesia was ineffective, then continuous deep sedation with the proportional side effect of unconsciousness could be justified. If a patient wanted to end their suffering by ending their life, then terminal anesthesia could also be justified. The harm in these cases is not unconsciousness and death but pain and suffering from being conscious. Sedation and anesthesia can eliminate this harm by eliminating its source gradually or rapidly. These claims are based not only on the patient's wishes but also their right to avoid distress and have some control over the time and manner of their death.

Intentional induction of permanent unconsciousness in terminal anesthesia seems more difficult to defend than continuous deep sedation because the goal is not palliation but death. It is controversial because pain and suffering could be controlled with continuous deep sedation, thus obviating the need for terminal anesthesia. Yet some patients may continue to feel pain and suffer in the initial stage of sedation. Rapid induction of unconsciousness until death may be necessary to avoid this. It would support an argument for terminal anesthesia over continuous palliative sedation. For those who consider death a harm, this action could be consistent with the principle of permissible harm in avoiding a state of affairs that would be worse for the patient.[221]

This raises the question of whether a physician would be obligated to provide terminal anesthesia to a patient if they requested it, or if a substitute decision-maker requested it on their behalf. Depending on how the physician interpreted their obligation to care for patients, and the unique circumstances and wishes of the patient, there could be latitude in how they discharged what is an imperfect obligation to provide specific interventions.[222] Terminal anesthesia may be compatible with this obligation. However, laws and best medical practices in different jurisdictions may restrict this as a treatment option. This implies that any right of a patient to proportional sedation or terminal anesthesia does not entail a perfect obligation for a physician to always fulfill a patient's request for these interventions.

Permanent unconsciousness is not equivalent to death. Yet if both states eliminate the capacity to feel pain and suffer, then they are not morally different in this respect. Sooner or later, death results from continuous palliative sedation or terminal anesthesia. A patient could remain unconscious and biologically alive for some time with continuous sedation. Because they could not have any negative experience, it would seem morally neutral if they remained in this state. But the UK judge's ruling in the PICU case of Pippa Knight mentioned earlier raises the question of whether artificially maintaining an adult patient in an unconscious state would burden them. This question could arise if, at an earlier time, a competent patient expressed an interest in not being kept alive after they had permanently lost consciousness. This could be a type of posthumous harm. It would be difficult to defend using scarce medical resources solely to keep a patient alive indefinitely when there was little or no chance of recovery to even a minimal level of awareness. One could make this claim even if an adult in a permanently unconscious state made an earlier request to remain biologically alive until all brain functions had permanently ceased, or if a family member made the request for them. These patient-based and resource-based considerations could support a shorter rather than longer period of unconsciousness leading to death and thus terminal anesthesia over continuous deep sedation.

Advanced disease can impair a patient's capacity to make decisions about continuous deep sedation or terminal anesthesia. This can preclude a clear and unambiguous request by the patient for either of these interventions. It can also preclude a request that they not receive them and remain conscious until the end of their life. These requests could be included in an advance directive by a patient expressing wishes about end-of-life care. In the absence of a directive or a request by a competent patient for sedation or anesthesia, proxies can decide for the patient based on their relationship with them and knowing which interventions the patient would or would not have wanted.[223] A patient's critical interest in remaining conscious, or being rendered unconscious, may have changed during the last stage of their life. When the patient's mental states are impaired, and there is no objective evidence of this change, a substitute decision to induce unconsciousness may fail to respect their interest. Similar remarks apply to a decision to maintain consciousness. Ideally, these issues would be discussed in exchanges between the patient and family when the patient was still competent. The attitudes they expressed in these exchanges could form a reliable basis on which others could make substitute decisions consistent with the patient's interests regarding whether their life should continue or whether and how it should end.[224]

Takla, Savulescu, and Wilkinson point out that "consciousness has instrumental value and is a means by which individuals realize their desires and intentions."[225] But they also claim that "a desire to no longer be conscious can also be rationalized on the view that consciousness has intrinsic value in a restricted sense."[226] "It is good overall when the positive aspects of consciousness outweigh the bad, rather than good in and of itself irrespective of what kind of experiences one is having."[227] The last part of this sentence suggests that the value at issue is not intrinsic but instrumental. If consciousness itself is not objectively but only subjectively good, or bad, depending on the nature and content of a person's experience, then its value is not intrinsic even in a restricted sense but only instrumental for the person who has it.

The authors defend their claim that intentionally causing unconsciousness at the end of life is compatible with the DDE and ethically justifiable:

> Consciousness in dying patients can already be compromised to an extent where it no longer provides the patient with valuable experiences, rendering further sedation morally neutral. Consciousness may also be unwanted and even feared in a dying patient, since the patient has a desire not to suffer, and has no remaining desires to remain aware and awake. In these circumstances, removing consciousness is not inherently bad (it is at worst morally neutral), and the DDE can therefore be used to justify its use. These arguments provide a defense for sedation at the end of life even where this comes at some risk of hastening death.[228]

They appear to be referring to continuous deep sedation aimed at palliation with death as an unintended side effect. For the reasons I have given, one could make a stronger claim and argument for intentionally and rapidly inducing unconsciousness with anesthesia until death. Whether this claim could be supported would depend on the patient's interest in remaining conscious or becoming unconscious. If consciousness had disvalue for them because it allowed them to feel pain and suffer, then removing consciousness would remove the ability to have these negative experiences. It would prevent continued harm to the patient. Because permanent unconsciousness would put the patient beyond harm, it would be morally neutral whether this state resulted from continuous deep sedation or terminal anesthesia. Both interventions could be morally permissible. The distinction between the physician's intention in administering sedation or anesthesia and knowing the outcome of these actions would not affect the permissibility of administering them if the patient wanted to end their conscious existence.

Some physicians administer terminal anesthesia when less radical palliative therapies would be sufficient to eliminate pain and suffering while allowing patients to remain conscious. Others would argue that this unnecessary and inappropriate use of terminal anesthesia fails to meet the DDE test. Describing it as "slow euthanasia" does not alter the fact that the goal of this intervention is to cause death. Nor does it diminish the ethically charged debate it has generated. Still, terminal anesthesia may become more ethically acceptable in light of the 2016 legalization of medical assistance in dying (MAID) in Canada and similar legislation in other jurisdictions.

## 9 Conclusion

Awareness enables us to deliberate, plan, and respond to reasons in adapting to and interacting with the natural and social environment. It generates the feeling of persisting through time and reflection on the experience of existing at different stages of life. Consciousness is at the core of questions in metaphysics and philosophy of mind about personhood, personal identity, and agency. These questions have normative implications. The capacity for experience gives us interests in the types of experience we want to have or avoid and grounds explanations for how we can benefit from or be harmed by them. The cognitive, affective, and volitional capacity to make conscious choices and perform intentional and voluntary actions entails taking responsibility and being held responsible for them.

Consciousness as such does not have ethical significance. Being aware is not intrinsically valuable but has value or disvalue depending on the subjective quality and content of our mental states, whether they are pleasurable or painful, and whether it enables us to meaningfully engage with others. The normative implications of consciousness are broad and include more than the issues I have discussed in this Element. But IA, prolonged DOCs, dissociative disorders, the role of consciousness in the neurological determination of death, and altering, restoring, and suppressing consciousness near the end of life generate the most ethically controversial issues among them. In some of these states, whether a person benefits or is harmed depends on whether they have phenomenal consciousness with, or without, access consciousness.

Explaining consciousness is not just a mind–brain problem. It is a mind–brain–body problem, where "body" is construed in an integrated way to include the body proper and central nervous, immune, endocrine, cardiovascular, and enteric nervous systems within the body. It also includes interoceptive, somatosensory, proprioceptive, and exteroceptive processes that connect these internal systems and the body to the external world.[229] Exteroception is just one aspect of how the brain and mind are influenced by the organism's and subject's adaptation to the environment. How the body is embedded in the environment influences how its internal processes shape neural and mental functions. Interactions between these systems and processes are critical to the phenomenology and content of consciousness, how it is generated and sustained, whether it is ordered or disordered, and how it influences our actions and their effects on ourselves and others.

What it is like subjectively to have experiential and critical interests and whether actions or other events realize or defeat these interests cannot be directly measured by neuroimaging, neural recording, or algorithms in interfacing systems. How awareness allows a person to benefit or be harmed and shapes their well-being can only be felt and known directly by that person. These are different aspects of the "hard" ethical problem of consciousness. Nevertheless, others may have indirect knowledge of these mental contents through a combination of imaging, recording, behavioral observation, social interaction, advance directives, and other measures. These can inform normative judgments about actions performed in altered or impaired conscious states. They can also provide guidance on how others should act to monitor, maintain, restore, or suppress consciousness at different stages of a person's life.

# Notes

1. Chalmers 1996.
2. McGinn 1989.
3. Chalmers 1995, 203.
4. Koch et al. 2016, 307.
5. Koch et al. 2016, 307; see also Crick & Koch 2003.
6. Feinberg 1984.
7. Parfit 1984, 493ff; Griffin 1986; Fletcher 2016.
8. Feinberg 1984, 91–5; Boonin 2019.
9. Zeman 2008, 314.
10. Frith 2008, 240.
11. Zeman 2008, 316.
12. Zeman 2008, 316.
13. Takla, Savulescu, & Wilkinson 2021, 287.
14. Glannon 2016.
15. Shepherd 2016.
16. Kahane & Savulescu 2009; Levy & Savulescu 2009; Wilkinson & Savulescu 2013.
17. Hawkins 2016; Wade 2017.
18. Levy 2014.
19. Takla, Savulescu, & Wilkinson 2021.
20. Posner et al. 2007.
21. Zeman 2008, 301; Northoff 2014, xvff.
22. Blumenfeld 2016a, 3.
23. Teasdale & Jennett 1974; Plum & Posner 1982; Blumenfeld 2016a, 6.
24. Mashour 2016.
25. Pal et al. 2018.
26. Tononi et al. 2016a, 423.
27. Crick & Koch 2003.
28. Baars 1988.
29. Dehaene & Changeux 2011.
30. Massimini & Tononi 2018, 63.
31. Tononi 2004; Tononi & Koch 2008; Tononi et al. 2016b.
32. Northoff & Huang 2017; Northoff 2018.
33. Northoff 2021, 67.
34. Northoff 2014, 247ff.
35. Tononi & Koch 2015.
36. Tononi & Koch 2008.
37. Mahner & Bunge 1997, 202ff; Koch 2019.
38. Koch 2019, xiv.
39. Feinberg 2001, 127–9; Feinberg & Mallatt 2018, 71–2.
40. Feinberg & Mallatt 2018, 71.
41. Koch 2019; Northoff 2014, 45.

42. Feinberg 2001.
43. Block 1995, 2007.
44. Block 1995, 227.
45. Block 1995, 227.
46. Owen et al. 2006; Owen & Coleman 2008; Owen 2019.
47. Schiff 2015; Claassen et al. 2019.
48. Levy 2013.
49. Mashour 2010, 2016; McKinstry-Wu & Kelz 2019.
50. Luppi et al. 2019.
51. Avidan, Mashour, & Glick 2009.
52. Avidan, Mashour, & Glick 2009.
53. Langsjo et al. 2012.
54. Tasbihgou, Vogels, & Absalom 2018.
55. Avidan et al. 2011.
56. Glannon 2019, 98ff.
57. Mashour & Alkire 2013; Mashour & Avidan 2015.
58. Tasbihgou, Vogels, & Absalom 2018.
59. Demertzi & Laureys 2012, 95.
60. Cassell 2004.
61. Langsjo et al. 2012; Kelz et al. 2019.
62. Naccache 2018.
63. Veselis 2015, i15.
64. Veselis 2015, i16.
65. Tulving & Schacter 1990; Eichenbaum 2012, 93.
66. Deeprose & Andrade 2006; Kihlstrom & Cork 2007.
67. Nowak et al. 2020.
68. Samuel et al. 2018.
69. Nowak et al. 2020, 1.
70. Nowak et al. 2020, 3.
71. Beauchamp & Childress 2019, Chs. 5, 6.
72. Laureys et al. 2010.
73. Multi-Society Task Force on PVS 1994.
74. Bernat 2006, 2010b.
75. Giacino et al. 2002, 2014.
76. Giacino et al. 2014, 101.
77. Giacino et al. 2014, 100.
78. Bernat 2006, 2010b.
79. Blumenfeld 2016b.
80. Giacino et al. 2002.
81. Giacino et al. 2014, 108.
82. Giacino et al. 2012.
83. Schnakers & Monti 2020.
84. Neville et al. 2019.
85. Vanhoecke & Hariz 2017.
86. Fins 2015.
87. Schiff et al. 2007.

88. Fins 2015, 233ff.
89. Chudy et al. 2018.
90. Graham et al. 2020.
91. Thibaut et al. 2019.
92. Young et al. 2021; Scolding, Owen, & Keown 2021; Cain et al. 2021.
93. Eskandar 2018.
94. Bernat 2010b.
95. Mathews, Fins, & Racine 2018.
96. Giacino et al. 2014, 107; Young, Bodien & Edlow, 2022.
97. Royal College of Physicians 2020.
98. Kahane & Savulescu 2009; Wilkinson & Savulescu 2013.
99. Graham & Naci 2021.
100. Schnakers 2016.
101. Celesia & Sannita 2013.
102. Boly et al. 2008; Demertzi & Laureys 2012.
103. Walsh 2012.
104. Giacino et al. 2014, 107.
105. Giacino et al. 2014.
106. Giacino et al. 2014, 109.
107. Fins 2005, 2015.
108. Birbaumer et al. 2014.
109. The Guardian 2012.
110. *Guy's and St. Thomas' Children's NHS Foundation Trust & Anor* v. *Knight & Anor* 2021.
111. Cited by Wilkinson 2021, 231.
112. Wilkinson & Savulescu 2013; Hawkins 2016.
113. Giacino et al. 2014, 110.
114. For example, *W* v. *M* 2011.
115. Peterson, Owen, & Karlawish 2020.
116. Owen 2019, 528; Moses et al. 2021.
117. Bernat 2020.
118. Monti et al. 2010.
119. Hochberg & Cudkowicz 2014, 1853.
120. Chaudhary et al. 2022.
121. Hochberg & Cash 2021, 279.
122. Morse 1994, 1642.
123. Cai & Bae 2020..
124. Zadra et al. 2013; Vesuna et al. 2020.
125. Dang-Vu et al. 2015.
126. Zadra et al. 2013, 289.
127. Solt & Akeju 2020.
128. Revonsuo, Kallio, & Sikka 2009, 187.
129. Spiegel & Cardena 1991.
130. Morse 1994, 1641-2, n. 146.
131. Morse 2016, 239.

132. M'Naghten's Case 1843/1975, 217; Model Penal Code 1985, 2.02; Schopp 1991; Morse 2010.
133. Fischer & Ravizza 1998, 28ff.
134. Frankfurt 1988; Mele 1995.
135. Morse 2016, 238.
136. Zadra et al. 2013, 292.
137. Zadra et al. 2013.
138. Zadra et al. 2013, 293.
139. *King* v. *Cogdon* 1950; Kadish & Schulhofer 2001, 193–5.
140. Moore 1984, 257.
141. Morse 1994, 1644–5.
142. Moore 2009.
143. Broughton et al. 1994.
144. *R* v. *Parks* 1992.
145. Bassetti 2016.
146. Levy 2014, 74.
147. Squire & Zola 1996.
148. Morse 2016, 238.
149. Vincent 2008, 2013.
150. Moore 2009, 183ff.
151. Sher 2009; Levy 2014.
152. Moore 2020, Pt. I.
153. Hallett 2007; Roskies 2010; Searle 2010.
154. De Haan, Rietveld, & Denys 2015.
155. President's Commission 1981, 73.
156. Pallis 1983.
157. Bernat 2010a, 246.
158. Bernat, Culver, & Gert 1981; Bernat 2002.
159. Greer et al. 2020.
160. Miller & Truog 2012, Chs. 3, 4.
161. Miller 2021.
162. Miller & Truog 2012.
163. Shewmon 1997, 68.
164. Shewmon 2001.
165. Veatch & Ross 2016, Ch. 5.
166. Tononi et al. 2016a.
167. McMahan 2002, 66ff.
168. DeGrazia 2005.
169. Dworkin 1993, 201–2.
170. Dworkin 1993, 202.
171. *Winkfield* v. *Children's Hospital Oakland* 2013.
172. *Cruzan* v. *Director, Missouri Department of Health* 1990.
173. Cited by McMahan 2002, 423.
174. Veatch & Ross 2016, 8.
175. Veatch & Ross 2016, 8.
176. Veatch & Ross 2016, 120ff.

177. Huang & Bernat 2019.
178. Johnston 1992.
179. Rodriguez-Arias, Smith, & Lazar 2011, 40.
180. Rodriguez-Arias, Smith, & Lazar 2011, 41.
181. Chon et al. 2014.
182. Miller, Truog, & Brock 2010.
183. Miller, Truog, & Brock 2010, 305.
184. Wilkinson & Savulescu 2012, 40–1.
185. Troppmann et al. 2019; Mezrich 2020.
186. Hosie et al. 2013; Maldonado 2015.
187. Milliere et al. 2018.
188. Oakley & Halligan 2013, 565.
189. Oakley & Halligan 2013, 568.
190. Deeley et al. 2012.
191. Wittmann 2013, 2016, 2018.
192. Oakley & Halligan 2013, 572.
193. Oakley & Halligan 2013, 572.
194. Cassell 2004, 281.
195. Damasio 1999, 75–6.
196. Tolstoy 1884–1886/2012, 53.
197. Tolstoy 1884–1886/2012, 53.
198. Wittgenstein 1921/1974, 6.4311.
199. Kamm 2013, 17–18.
200. Kamm 2013, 17.
201. Johnston 2010, 175.
202. Grob et al. 2011.
203. Ballard & Zarate 2020.
204. Ross et al. 2016.
205. Carhart-Harris et al. 2017.
206. Smith & Sisti 2021.
207. Wittmann 2016, 105ff.
208. Martial et al. 2021.
209. Kocarova, Horacek, & Carhart-Harris 2021.
210. Cited by Griffin 1986, 8.
211. Takla, Savulescu, & Wilkinson 2021, 284, 286.
212. Wiffen, Derry, & Moore 2014.
213. Woodward 2001; Cavanagh 2006; Kamm 2020, Ch. 7.
214. Wittgenstein 1921/1974, 6.4311.
215. Kamm 2020, 194.
216. Steinbock & Norcross 1994.
217. Sulmasy 2018, 239ff.
218. Sulmasy 2018, 235.
219. Sulmasy 2018, 240.
220. Raus, Sterckx, & Mortier 2013.
221. Kamm 2007, 24ff.
222. Kant 1785/1964.

223. Takla, Savulescu, & Wilkinson 2021, 289.
224. Kamm 2020, Ch. 4.
225. Takla, Savulescu, & Wilkinson 2021, 288.
226. Takla, Savulescu, & Wilkinson 2021, 288.
227. Takla, Savulescu, & Wilkinson 2021, 288.
228. Takla, Savulescu, & Wilkinson 2021, 291.
229. Northoff 2018, 2021.

# References

Avidan, Michael, Mashour, George, and Glick, David. Prevention of Awareness During General Anesthesia. *F1000 Medicine Reports* 1 (2009): 9. http://doi.org.10.3410/MI-9.

Avidan, Michael, Jacobsohn, Eric, Glick, David et al. Prevention of Intraoperative Awareness in a High-Risk Surgical Population. *New England Journal of Medicine* 365 (2011): 591–600.

Baars, Bernard. *A Cognitive Theory of Consciousness*. Cambridge: Cambridge University Press, 1988.

Ballard, Elizabeth, and Zarate, Carlos. The Role of Dissociation in Ketamine's Antidepressant Effects. *Nature Communications* 11 (2020): 6431. http://doi.org/10.1038/s41467-020-20190-4.

Bassetti, Claudio. Sleepwalking: Dissociation between "Body Sleep" and "Mind Sleep." In Laureys, Gosseries, and Tononi (eds.), 2016, pp. 129–38.

Baumeister, Roy, Mele, Alfred, and Vohs, Kathleen, eds. *Free Will and Consciousness: How Might They Work?* New York: Oxford University Press, 2010.

Beauchamp, Tom, and Childress, James. *Principles of Biomedical Ethics*, 8th ed. New York: Oxford University Press, 2019.

Bernat, James. The Biophilosophical Basis of Whole-Brain Death. In Paul, Miller, and Paul (eds.), 2002, pp. 324–42.

Bernat, James. Chronic Disorders of Consciousness. *The Lancet* 367 (2006): 1181–92.

Bernat, James. How the Distinction between "Irreversible" and "Permanent" Illuminates Circulatory Respiratory Death Determination. *Journal of Medicine and Philosophy* 35 (2010a): 242–55.

Bernat, James. The Natural History of Chronic Disorders of Consciousness. *Neurology* 75 (2010b): 206–7.

Bernat, James. Medical Decision Making by Patients in the Locked-In Syndrome. *Neuroethics* 13 (2020): 229–38.

Bernat, James, Culver, Charles, and Gert, Bernard. On the Definition and Criterion of Death. *Annals of Internal Medicine* 94 (1981): 389–94.

Birbaumer, Niels, Gallegos-Ayala, Guillermo, Wildgruber, Moritz et al. Direct Brain Control and Communication in Paralysis. *Brain Topography* 27 (2014): 4–11.

Block, Ned. On a Confusion About a Function of Consciousness. *Behavioral and Brain Sciences* 18 (1995): 227–87.

Block, Ned. Consciousness, Accessibility and the Mesh between Psychology and Neuroscience. *Behavioral and Brain Sciences* 30 (2007): 481–99.

Blumenfeld, Hal. Neuroanatomical Basis of Consciousness. In Laureys, Gosseries, and Tononi (eds.), 2016a, pp. 3–29.

Blumenfeld, Hal. Epilepsy and Consciousness. In Laureys, Gosseries, and Tononi (eds.), 2016b, pp. 255–70.

Boly, Melanie, Faymonville, Marie-Elisabeth, Schnakers, Caroline et al. Perception of Pain in the Minimally Conscious State with PET Activation: An Observational Study. *The Lancet Neurology* 7 (2008): 1013–20.

Boonin, David. *Dead Wrong: The Ethics of Posthumous Harm.* New York: Oxford University Press, 2019.

Broughton, Roger, Billings, Rodger, Cartwright, Rosalind et al. Homicidal Somnambulism: A Case Report. *Sleep: Journal of Sleep Research and Sleep Medicine* 17 (1994): 253–64.

Cai, Alice, and Bae, Charles. Parasomnias. In Cucchiara and Price (eds.), 2020, pp. 164–5.

Cain, Joshua, Spivak, Norman, Coetzee, John et al. Ultrasonic Thalamic Stimulation in Chronic Disorders of Consciousness. *Brain Stimulation* 14 (2021): 301-3

Carhart-Harris, Robin, Roseman, Leor, Bolstridge, Mark et al. Psilocybin for Treatment-Resistant Depression: fMRI-Measured Brain Mechanisms. *Scientific Reports* 7 (2017): 13187. http://doi.org/10.1035/srep41598-017-13282-7.

Cassell, Eric. *The Nature of Suffering and the Goals of Medicine*, 2nd ed. New York: Oxford University Press, 2004.

Cavanagh, Thomas. *Double Effect: Doing Good and Avoiding Evil.* Oxford: Clarendon Press, 2006.

Celesia, Gaston, and Sannita, Walter. Can Patients in Vegetative State Experience Pain and Have Conscious Awareness? *Neurology* 80 (2013): 328–9.

Chalmers, David. Facing Up to the Problem of Consciousness. *Journal of Consciousness Studies* 2 (1995): 200–19.

Chalmers, David. *The Conscious Mind: In Search of a Fundamental Theory.* New York: Oxford University Press, 1996.

Chaudhary, Ujwal, Vlachos, Ioannis, Zimmermann, Jonas et al. Spelling Interface Using Intracortical Signals in a Completely Locked-In Patient Enabled via Auditory Neurofeedback Training. *Nature Communications* 13 (2022): 1236. http://doi.org/10.1038/s41467-022-288598.

Chon, W. James, Josephson, Michelle, Gordon, Elise et al. When the Living and the Deceased Cannot Agree on Organ Donation: A Survey of US Organ

Procurement Organizations (OPOs). *American Journal of Transplantation* 14 (2014): 172–7.

Chudy, Darko, Deletis, Vedran, Almahariq, Fadi et al. Deep Brain Stimulation for the Early Treatment of the Minimally Conscious State and Vegetative State: Experience in 14 Patients. *Journal of Neurosurgery* 128 (2018): 1189–98.

Claassen, Jan, Doyle, Kevin, Matory, Adu et al. Detection of Brain Activation in Unresponsive Patients with Acute Brain Injury. *New England Journal of Medicine* 380 (2019): 2497–505.

Crick, Francis, and Koch, Christof. A Framework for Consciousness. *Nature Neuroscience* 6 (2003): 119–26.

*Cruzan v. Director, Missouri Department of Health*, 1990.

Cucchiara, Brett, and Price, Raymond, eds. *Decision-Making in Adult Neurology*. Amsterdam: Elsevier, 2020.

Damasio, Antonio. *The Feeling of What Happens: Body and Emotion in the Making of Consciousness*. Orlando, FL: Harcourt Brace, 1999.

Dang-Vu, Thien, Zadra, Antonio, Labelle, Marc-Antoine et al. Sleep Deprivation Reveals Altered Brain Perfusion Patterns in Somnambulism. *PLoS One* 10 (2015): 0133474. http://doi.org/10.1371/journal.pone.0133474.

Deeley, Quinton, Oakley, David, Toone, Brian et al. Modulating the Default Mode Network Using Hypnosis. *International Journal of Clinical and Experimental Hypnosis* 60 (2012): 206–28.

Deeprose, Catherine, and Andrade, Jackie. Is Priming during Anesthesia Unconscious? *Consciousness and Cognition* 15 (2006): 1–23.

DeGrazia, David. *Human Identity and Bioethics*. New York: Cambridge University Press, 2005.

De Haan, Sanneke, Rietveld, Erik, and Denys, Damiaan. Being Free by Losing Control: What Obsessive-Compulsive Disorder Can Tell Us About Free Will. In Glannon (ed.), 2015, pp. 83–102.

Dehaene, Stanislas, and Changeux, Jean-Pierre. Experimental and Theoretical Approaches to Conscious Processing. *Neuron* 70 (2011): 200–27.

Demertzi, Athena, and Laureys, Steven. Where in the Brain Is Pain? Evaluating Painful Experiences in Non-Communicative Patients. In Richmond, Rees, and Edwards (eds.), 2012, pp. 89–98.

Dworkin, Ronald. *Life's Dominion: An Argument About Abortion, Euthanasia, and Individual Freedom*.

Eichenbaum, Howard. *The Cognitive Neuroscience of Memory: An Introduction*, 2nd ed. New York: Oxford University Press, 2012.

Eskandar, Emad. Thalamic Stimulation in Vegetative or Minimally Conscious Patients. *Journal of Neurosurgery* 128 (2018): 1187–88.

Feinberg, Joel. *Harm to Others*. New York: Oxford University Press, 1984.

Feinberg, Todd. *Altered Egos: How the Brain Creates the Self.* New York: Oxford University Press, 2001.

Feinberg, Todd, and Mallatt, Jon. *Consciousness Demystified.* Cambridge, MA: MIT Press, 2018.

Ferzan, Kimberly, and Morse, Stephen, eds. *Legal, Moral, and Metaphysical Truths: The Philosophy of Michael Moore.* New York: Oxford University Press, 2016.

Fins, Joseph. Rethinking Disorders of Consciousness: New Research and its Implications. *Hastings Center Report* 35 (2) (2005): 22–4.

Fins, Joseph. *Rights Come to Mind: Brain Injury, Ethics, and the Struggle for Consciousness.* New York: Cambridge University Press, 2015.

Fischer, John Martin, and Ravizza, Mark. *Responsibility and Control: A Theory of Moral Responsibility.* New York: Cambridge University Press, 1998.

Fletcher, Guy. *The Philosophy of Well-Being: An Introduction.* New York: Routledge, 2016.

Fogel, Barry, and Greenberg, Donna, eds. *Psychiatric Care of the Medical Patient*, 3rd ed. Oxford: Oxford University Press, 2015.

Frankfurt, Harry. Identification and Externality. In *The Important of What We Care About.* New York: Cambridge University Press, 1988, pp. 58–68.

Freeman, Michael, ed. *Law and Neuroscience.* Oxford: Oxford University Press, 2010.

Frith, Chris. The Social Functions of Consciousness. In Weiskrantz and Davies (eds.), 2008, pp. 225–44.

Giacino, Joseph, Ashwal, Stephen, Childs, Nancy et al. The Minimally Conscious State: Definition and Diagnostic Criteria. *Neurology* 58 (2002): 349–53.

Giacino, Joseph, Whyte, John, Bagiella, Emilia et al. Placebo-Controlled Trial of Amantadine for Severe Traumatic Brain Injury. *New England Journal of Medicine* 366 (2012): 819–26.

Giacino, Joseph, Fins, Joseph, Laureys, Steven, and Schiff, Nicholas. Disorders of Consciousness after Acquired Brain Injury: The State of the Science. *Nature Reviews Neurology* 10 (2014): 99–114.

Glannon, Walter, ed. *Free Will and the Brain: Neuroscientific, Philosophical and Legal Perspectives.* Cambridge: Cambridge University Press, 2015.

Glannon, Walter. The Value and Disvalue of Consciousness. *Cambridge Quarterly of Healthcare Ethics* 25 (2016): 600–12.

Glannon, Walter. *The Neuroethics of Memory: From Total Recall to Oblivion.* Cambridge: Cambridge University Press, 2019.

Graham, Mackenzie, and Naci, Lorina. Well-Being after Severe Brain Injury: What Counts as Good Recovery? *Cambridge Quarterly of Healthcare Ethics* 30 (2021): 613–22.

Graham, Neil, Jolly, Amy, Zimmerman, Karl et al. Diffuse Axonal Injury Predicts Neurodegeneration after Moderate-Severe Traumatic Brain Injury. *Brain* 143 (2020): 3685-98.

Greer, David, Shemie, Sam, Lewis, Ariane et al. Determination of Brain Death/ Death by Neurologic Criteria: The World Brain Death Project. *Journal of the American Medical Association* 324 (2020): 1078–97.

Griffin, James. *Well-Being: Its Meaning, Measurement and Moral Importance.* Oxford: Clarendon Press, 1986.

Grob, Charles, Danforth, Alicia, Chopra, Gurpreet et al. Pilot Study of Psilocybin Treatment for Anxiety in Patients with Advanced-Stage Cancer. *Archives of General Psychiatry* 68 (2011): 71–8.

*Guy's and St. Thomas' Children's NHS Foundation Trust & Anor* v. *Knight & Anor.* EWHC 25 (Fam), 2021.

Hallett, Michael. Volitional Control of Movement: The Physiology of Free Will. *Clinical Neurophysiology* 11 (2007): 79–92.

Hawkins, Jennifer. What Is Good *for Them*? Best Interests and Severe Disorders of Consciousness. In Sinnott-Armstrong (ed.), 2016, pp. 180–206.

Hochberg, Leigh, and Cash, Sydney. Freedom of Speech. *New England Journal of Medicine* 385 (2021): 278–9.

Hochberg, Leigh, and Cudkowicz, Merit. Locked In, but Not Out? *Neurology* 82 (2014): 1852–3.

Hosie, Annmarie, Davidson, Patricia, Agar, Meera et al. Delirium: Prevalence, Incidence, and Implications for Screening in Specialist Palliative Care Inpatient Settings: A Systematic Review. *Palliative Medicine* 27 (2013): 486–98.

Huang, Andrew, and Bernat, James. The Organism as a Whole in an Analysis of Death. *Journal of Medicine and Philosophy* 44 (2019): 712–31.

Johnston, Mark. Constitution Is Not Identity. *Mind* 101 (1992): 89–106.

Johnston, Mark. *Surviving Death*. Princeton: Princeton University Press, 2010.

Kadish, Sanford, and Schulhofer, Stephen. *Criminal Law and Its Processes: Cases and Materials*, 8th ed. New York: Aspen, 2001.

Kahane, Guy, and Savulescu, Julian. Brain Damage and the Moral Significance of Consciousness. *Journal of Medicine and Philosophy* 34 (2009): 6–26.

Kamm, Frances. *Intricate Ethics: Rights, Responsibility, and Permissible Harm.* Oxford: Oxford University Press, 2007.

Kamm, Frances. Rescuing Ivan Ilych: How We Live and How We Die In *Bioethical Prescriptions: To Create, End, Choose, and Improve Lives.* Oxford: Oxford University Press, 2013, pp. 3–32.

Kamm, Frances. *Almost Over: Aging, Dying, Dead.* Oxford: Oxford University Press, 2020.

Kant, Immanuel. *Groundwork of the Metaphysics of Morals*, trans. H. J. Paton. New York: Harper & Row, 1785/1964.

Kelz, Max, Garcia, Paul, Mashour, George and Solt, Ken. Escape from Oblivion: Neural Mechanisms of Emergence from General Anesthesia. *Anesthesia and Analgesia* 128 (2019): 726–36.

Kihlstrom, John, and Cork, Randall. Consciousness and Anesthesia. In Velmans and Schneider (eds.), 2007, pp. 628–39.

*King* v. *Cogdon*. Supreme Court of Victoria, Australia, 1950.

Kocarova, Rita, Horacek, Jiri, and Carhart-Harris, Robin. Does Psilocybin Have a Transdiagnostic Action and Prophylactic Potential? *Frontiers in Psychiatry* 12 (2021): 233. http://doi.org/10.3389/fpsyt.2021.661233.

Koch, Christof. *The Feeling of Life Itself: Why Consciousness Is Widespread but Can't Be Computed*. Cambridge, MA: MIT Press, 2019.

Koch, Christof, Massimini, Marcello, Boly, Melanie, and Tononi, Giulio. Neural Correlates of Consciousness: Progress and Problems. *Nature Reviews Neuroscience* 17 (2016): 307–21.

Langsjo, Jaakko, Alkire, Michael, Kaskinoro, Kimmo et al. Returning from Oblivion: Imaging the Neural Core of Consciousness. *Journal of Neuroscience* 32 (2012): 4935–43.

Laureys, Steven, Celesia, Gastone, Cohadon, Francois et al. Unresponsive Wakefulness Syndrome: A New Name for the Vegetative State or Apallic syndrome. *BMC Medicine* 8 (2010): 68. http://doi.org/10.1186/1741-7015-8-68.

Laureys, Steven, Gosseries, Olivia, and Tononi, Giulio, eds. *The Neurology of Consciousness: Cognitive Neuroscience and Neuropathology*, 2nd ed. Amsterdam: Elsevier Academic Press, 2016.

Levy, Neil. The Importance of Awareness. *Australasian Journal of Philosophy* 91 (2013): 2011–29.

Levy, Neil. *Consciousness and Moral Responsibility*. Oxford: Oxford University Press, 2014.

Levy, Neil, and Savulescu, Julian. Moral Significance of Phenomenal Consciousness. *Progress in Brain Research* 177 (2009): 361–70.

Luppi, Andrea, Craig, Michael, Pappas, Ioannis et al. Consciousness-Specific Dynamic Interactions of Brain Integration and Functional Diversity. *Nature Communications* 10 (2019): 4616. http://doi.org/10.1038/s41467-019-12658-9.

Mahner, Martin, and Bunge, Mario. *Foundations of Biophilosophy*. Berlin: Springer-Verlag, 1997.

Maldonado, Jose. Delirium: Neurobiology, Characteristics and Management. In Fogel and Greenberg (eds.), 2015. http://doi.org/10.1093/med/9780199731855.003.0041, 1-218.

Martial, Charlotte, Fontaine, Geraldine, Gosseries, Olivia et al. Losing the Self in Near-Death Experiences: The Experience of Ego-Dissolution. *Brain Sciences* 11 (2021): 929. http://doi.org/10.3390/brainsci11070929.

Mashour, George, ed. *Consciousness, Awareness, and Anesthesia.* New York: Cambridge University Press, 2010.

Mashour, George. Consciousness and Anesthesia. In Laureys, Gosseries, and Tononi (eds.), 2016, pp. 139–54.

Mashour, George, and Alkire, Michael. Consciousness, Anesthesia, and the Thalamocortical System. *Anesthesiology* 118 (2013): 13-15.

Mashour, George, and Avidan, Michael. Intraoperative Awareness: Controversies and Non-Controversies. *British Journal of Anaesthesia* 112 (2015): i20–i26.

Mashour, George, and Engelhard, Kristin, eds. *Oxford Textbook of Neuroscience and Anaesthesiology.* Oxford: Oxford University Press, 2019.

Massimini, Marcello, and Tononi, Giulio. *Sizing Up Consciousness: Towards an Objective Measure of the Capacity for Experience.* Oxford: Oxford University Press, 2018.

Mathews, Debra, Fins, Joseph, and Racine, Eric. The Therapeutic "Mis" Conception: An Examination of its Normative Assumptions and a Call for its Revision. *Cambridge Quarterly of Healthcare Ethics* 27 (2018): 154–62.

McGinn, Colin. Can We Solve the Mind-Body Problem? *Mind* 98 (1989): 349–66.

McKinstry-Wu, Andrew, and Kelz, Max. Neural Mechanisms of Anaesthetics. In Mashour and Engelhard (eds.), 2019, pp. 3–14.

McMahan, Jeff. *The Ethics of Killing: Problems at the Margins of Life.* Oxford: Oxford University Press, 2002.

Mele, Alfred. *Autonomous Agents: From Self-Control to Autonomy.* New York: Cambridge University Press, 1995.

Mezrich, Joshua. Altruism *in Extremis* – The Evolving Ethics of Organ Donation. *New England Journal of Medicine* 382 (2020): 493–6.

Miller, Franklin. Individuals Declared Brain-Dead Remain Biologically Alive. *Hastings Bioethics Forum*, October 28, 2021. www.thehastingscenter.org.brain-death/.

Miller, Franklin, and Truog, Robert. *Death, Dying and Organ Transplantation: Reconstructing Medical Ethics at the End of Life.* New York: Oxford University Press, 2012.

Miller, Franklin, Truog, Robert, and Brock, Dan. The Dead Donor Rule: Can it Withstand Critical Scrutiny? *Journal of Medicine and Philosophy* 35 (2010): 299–312.

Milliere, Raphael, Carhart-Harris, Robin, Roseman, Leor et al. Psychedelics, Meditation, and Self-Consciousness. *Frontiers in Psychology* 9 (2018): 1475. http://doi.org/10.3389/fpsyg.2018.01475.

M'Naghten's Case. Cited in the Report of the Committee on Mentally Abnormal Offenders. London: Her Majesty's Stationery Office, 1843/ 1975.

Model Penal Code. Official Draft and Commentaries. Philadelphia: American Law Institute, 1985.

Monti, Martin, Vanhaudenhuyse, Audrey, Coleman, Martin et al. Willful Modulation of Brain Activity in Disorders of Consciousness. *New England Journal of Medicine* 362 (2010): 579–89.

Moore, Michael. *Law and Psychiatry: Rethinking the Relationship*. New York: Cambridge University Press, 1984.

Moore, Michael. *Causation and Responsibility: An Essay in Law, Morals, and Metaphysics*. New York: Oxford University Press, 2009.

Moore, Michael. *Mechanical Choices: The Responsibility of the Human Machine*. New York: Oxford University Press, 2020.

Morse, Stephen. Culpability and Control. *University of Pennsylvania Law Review* 142 (1994): 1587–660.

Morse, Stephen. Lost in Translation? An Essay on Law and Neuroscience. In Freeman (ed.), 2010, pp. 529–62.

Morse, Stephen. Moore on the Mind. In Ferzan and Morse (eds.), 2016, pp. 233–49.

Moses, David, Metzger, Sean, Liu, Jessie et al. Neuroprosthesis for Decoding Speech in a Paralyzed Person with Anarthria. *New England Journal of Medicine* 385 (2021): 217–27.

Multi-Society Task Force on PVS. Medical Aspects of the Persistent Vegetative State. *New England Journal of Medicine* 330 (1994): 1499–508.

Naccache, Lionel. Why and How Access Consciousness Can Account for Phenomenal Consciousness. *Philosophical Transactions of the Royal Society B: Biological Sciences* 373 (2018): 357. http://doi.org/10.1098/rstb.2017.0357.

Neville, Iuri, Zaninotto, Ana, Hayashi, Cintya et al. Repetitive TMS Does not Improve Cognition in Patients with TBI. *Neurology* 93 (2019): e190–e199.

Northoff, Georg. *Unlocking the Brain, Volume II: Consciousness*. New York: Oxford University Press, 2014.

Northoff, Georg. *The Spontaneous Brain: From the Mind-Body to the World-Brain Problem*. Cambridge, MA: MIT Press, 2018.

Northoff, Georg. Why Is There Sentience? A Temporo-Spatial Approach to Consciousness. *Journal of Consciousness Studies* 28 (2021): 67–82.

Northoff, Georg, and Huang, Zirui. How Do the Brain's Time and Space Mediate Consciousness and Its Different Dimensions? Temporo-Spatial Theory of Consciousness (TTC). *Neuroscience & Biobehavioral Reviews* 80 (2017): 630–45.

Nowak, Hartmuth, Zech, Nina, Asmussen, Sven et al. Effect of Therapeutic Suggestions during General Anaesthesia on Postoperative Pain and Opioid Use: Multicentre Randomised Controlled Trial. *BMJ* 371 (2020): m4284. http://doi.org/10.1136/bmj.m4284.

Oakley, David, and Halligan, Peter. Hypnotic Suggestion: Opportunities for Cognitive Neuroscience. *Nature Reviews Neuroscience* 14 (2013): 565–76.

Owen, Adrian. The Search for Consciousness. *Neuron* 102 (2019): 526–8.

Owen, Adrian, and Coleman, Martin. Functional Neuroimaging of the Vegetative State. *Nature Reviews Neuroscience* 9 (2008): 235–43.

Owen, Adrian, Coleman, Martin, Boly, Melanie et al. Detecting Awareness in the Vegetative State. *Science* 313 (2006): 1402.

Pal, Dinesh, Dean, Jon, Liu, Tiecheng et al. Differential Role of Prefrontal and Parietal Cortices in Controlling Level of Consciousness. *Current Biology* 28 (2018): 2145–52.

Pallis, Christopher. ABC of Brainstem Death: The Declaration of Death. *BMJ* 286 (1983): 39.

Parfit, Derek. *Reasons and Persons*. Oxford: Clarendon Press, 1984.

Paul, Ellen Frankel, Miller, Fred, and Paul, Jeffrey, eds. *Bioethics*. New York: Cambridge University Press, 2002.

Peterson, Andrew, Owen, Adrian, and Karlawish, Jason. Alive Inside. *Bioethics* 34 (2020): 295–305.

Plum, Fred, and Posner, Jerome. *The Diagnosis of Stupor and Coma*, 3rd ed. Philadelphia: F. A. Davis, 1982.

Posner, Jerome, Saper, Christopher, Schiff, Nicholas, and Plum, Fred. *Plum and Posner's Diagnosis of Stupor and Coma*, 4th ed. New York: Oxford University Press, 2007.

President's Commission for the Study of Ethical Problems in Medicine and Biomedical and Behavioral Research (US). *Defining Death: Medical, Legal and Ethical Issues in the Determination of Death*. Washington, DC: US Government Printing Office, 1981.

*R* v. *Parks*. 2 S.C.R. 871, Supreme Court of Canada, 1992.

Raus, Kasper, Sterckx, Sigrid, and Mortier, Freddy. Can the Doctrine of Double Effect Justify Continuous Deep Sedation at the End of Life? In Sterckx, Raus, and Mortier (eds.), 2013, pp. 177–201.

Revonsuo, Antti, Kallio, Sakari, and Sikka, Pilleriin. What Is an Altered State of Consciousness? *Philosophical Psychology* 22 (2009): 187–204.

Richmond, Sarah, Rees, Geraint, and Edwards, Sarah, eds. *I Know What You're Thinking: Brain Imaging and Mental Privacy.* Oxford: Oxford University Press, 2012.

Rodriguez-Arias, David, Smith, Maxwell, and Lazar, Neil. Donation after Circulatory Death: Burying the Dead Donor Rule. *American Journal of Bioethics* 11 (2011): 36–43.

Roskies, Adina. Freedom, Neural Mechanism and Consciousness. In Baumeister, Mele, and Vohs (eds.), 2010, pp. 153–71.

Ross, Stephen, Bossis, Anthony, Guss, Jeffrey et al. Rapid and Sustained Symptom Reduction Following Psilocybin Treatment for Anxiety and Depression in Patients with Life-Threatening Cancer: A Randomized Controlled Trial. *Journal of Psychopharmacology* 30 (2016): 1165–80.

Royal College of Physicians. Prolonged Disorders of Consciousness Following Sudden Onset Brain Injury: National Clinical Guidelines. 2020. https://www.rcplondon.ac.uk/guidelines-policy/prolonged-disorders-consciousness-follow ing-sudden-onset-braininjury-national-clinical-guidelines.

Samuel, Nir, Taub, Aryeh, Paz, Rony, and Raz, Aeyal. Implicit Aversive Memory under Anaesthesia in Animal Models: A Narrative Review. *British Journal of Anaesthesia* 121 (2018): 219–32.

Schiff, Nicholas. Cognitive Motor Dissociation Following Severe Brain Injuries. *JAMA Neurology* 72 (2015): 1413–15.

Schiff, Nicholas, Giacino, Joseph, Kalmar, Kathy et al. Behavioural Improvements with Thalamic Stimulation after Severe Traumatic Brain Injury. *Nature* 448 (2007): 600-3.

Schnakers, Caroline. What Is It Like to Be in a Disorder of Consciousness? In Sinnott-Armstrong (ed.), 2016, pp. 83–99.

Schnakers, Caroline, and Monti, Martin. Towards Improving Care for Disorders of Consciousness. *Nature Reviews Neurology* 16 (2020): 405–6.

Schopp, Robert. *Automatism, Insanity, and the Psychology of Criminal Responsibility: A Philosophical Inquiry.* New York: Cambridge University Press, 1991.

Scolding, Neil, Owen, Adrian, and Keown, John. Prolonged Disorders of Consciousness: A Critical Evaluation of the New UK Guidelines. *Brain* 144 (2021): 1655–60.

Searle, John. Consciousness and the Problem of Free Will. In Baumeister, Mele, and Vohs (eds.), 2010, pp. 121–34.

Shepherd, Joshua. Moral Conflict in the Minimally Conscious State. In Sinnott-Armstrong (ed.), 2016, pp. 160–79.

Shepherd, Joshua. *Consciousness and Moral Status.* New York: Routledge, 2018.

Sher, George. *Who Knew? Responsibility without Awareness*. New York: Oxford University Press, 2009.

Shewmon, Alan. Recovery from "Brain Death": A Neurologist's Apologia. *Linacre Quarterly* 64 (1997): 30–96.

Shewmon, Alan. The Brain and Somatic Integration: Insights into the Standard Biological Rationale for Equating "Brain Death" with Death. *Journal of Medicine and Philosophy* 26 (2001): 457–78.

Sinnott-Armstrong, Walter, ed. *Finding Consciousness: The Neuroscience, Ethics and Law of Severe Brain Damage*. New York: Oxford University Press, 2016.

Smith, William, and Sisti, Dominic. Ethics and Ego Dissolution: The Case of Psilocybin. *Journal of Medical Ethics* 47 (2021): 807–14.

Solt, Ken, and Akeju, Oluwaseun. An Altered State of Consciousness Illuminated. *Nature* 586 (2020): 31–2.

Spiegel, David, and Cardena, Etzel. Disintegrated Experience: The Dissociative Disorders Revisited. *Journal of Abnormal Psychology* 100 (1991): 366–78.

Squire, Larry, and Zola, Stuart. Structure and Function of Declarative and Non-Declarative Memory Systems. *Proceedings of the National Academy of Sciences* 93 (1996): 13515–22.

Steinbock, Bonnie, and Norcross, Alastair, eds. *Killing and Letting Die*, 2nd ed. New York: Fordham University Press, 1994.

Sterckx, Sigrid, Raus, Kasper, and Mortier, Freddy, eds. *Continuous Sedation at the End of Life: Ethical, Clinical and Legal Perspectives*. Cambridge: Cambridge University Press, 2013.

Sulmasy, Daniel. The Last Low Whispers of Our Dead: When Is it Ethically Justifiable to Render a Patient Unconscious Until Death? *Theoretical Medicine and Bioethics* 39 (2018): 233–63.

Takla, Antony, Savulescu, Julian, and Wilkinson, Dominic. A Conscious Choice: Is it Ethical to Aim for Unconsciousness at the End of Life? *Bioethics* 35 (2021): 284–91.

Tasbihgou, Setayesh, Vogels, M. F., and Absalom, Anthony. Accidental Awareness during General Anesthesia: A Narrative Review. *Anaesthesia* 73 (2018): 112–22.

Teasdale, Graham, and Jennett, Bryan. Assessment of Coma and Impaired Consciousness. *The Lancet* 303 (1974): 81–4.

The Guardian. Report on the Right-to-Die Case of LIS Patient Tony Nicklinson. August 22, 2012. http://theguardian.com/uk/2012/august/22/tony-nicklinson-right-to-die-case.

Thibaut, Aurore, Schiff, Nicholas, Giacino, Joseph, Laureys, Steven, and Gosseries, Olivia. Therapeutic Interventions in Patients with Prolonged Disorders of Consciousness. *The Lancet Neurology* 18 (2019): 600–14.

Tolstoy, Lev. *The Death of Ivan Ilych*, trans. R. Pevear and L. Volokhonsky. New York: Random House, 1884–1886/2012.

Tononi, Giulio. An Information Integration Theory of Consciousness. *BMC Neuroscience* 5 (2004): 42. http://doi.org/10.1186/1471-2202-5-42.

Tononi, Giulio, and Koch, Christof. The Neural Correlates of Consciousness: An Update. *Annals of the New York Academy of Sciences* 1124 (2008): 239–61.

Tononi, Giulio, and Koch, Christof. Consciousness: Here, There and Everywhere? *Philosophical Transactions of the Royal Society B* 370 (2015): 20140167. http://doi.org/10.1098/rstb.2014.0167.

Tononi, Giulio, Boly, Melanie, Gosseries, Olivia, and Laureys, Steven. The Neurology of Consciousness: An Overview. In Laureys, Gosseries, and Tononi (eds.), 2016a, pp. 407–61.

Tononi, Giulio, Boly, Melanie, Massimini, Marcello, and Koch, Christof. Integrated Information Theory: From Consciousness to its Physical Substrate. *Nature Reviews Neuroscience* 17 (2016b): 450–61.

Troppmann, Christoph, Santhanakrishnan, Chandrasekar, Segeshima, Junichiro et al . Barriers to Live and Deceased Kidney Donation by Patients with Chronic Neurological Diseases: Implications for Donor Selection, Donation Timing, Logistics, and Regulatory Compliance. *American Journal of Transplantation* 19 (2019): 2168–73.

Tulving, Endel, and Schacter, Daniel. Priming and Human Memory Systems. *Science* 247 (1990): 301–6.

Vanhoecke, Jonathan, and Hariz, Marwan. Deep Brain Stimulation for Disorders of Consciousness: Systematic Review of Cases and Ethics. *Brain Stimulation* 10 (2017): 113–23.

Veatch, Robert. The Death of Whole-Brain Death: The Plague of the Disaggregators, Somaticists, and Mentalists. *Journal of Medicine and Philosophy* 30 (2005): 353–78.

Veatch, Robert, and Ross, Lainie Friedman. *Defining Death: The Case for Choice*. Washington, DC: Georgetown University Press, 2016.

Velmans, Max, and Schneider, Susan, eds. *The Blackwell Companion to Consciousness*. Malden: Blackwell, 2007.

Veselis, Robert. Memory Formation During Anaesthesia: Plausibility of a Neurophysiological Basis. *British Journal of Anaesthesia* 115 (2015): i13-i19.

Vesuna, Sam, Kauvar, Isaac, Richman, Ethan et al. Deep Posteromedial Cortical Rhythm in Dissociation. *Nature* 586 (2020): 87–94.

Vincent, Nicole. Responsibility, Dysfunction and Capacity. *Neuroethics* 1 (2008): 199–204.

Vincent, Nicole. Blame, Desert and Compatibilist Capacity: A Diachronic Account of Moderateness in Regard to Reasons-Responsiveness. *Philosophical Explorations* 6 (2013): 178–94.

*W* v. *M*. EWHC 2443 (Fam), 2011.

Wade, Derick. Back to the Bedside? Making Clinical Decisions in Patients with Prolonged Unconsciousness. *Journal of Medical Ethics* 43 (2017): 439–45.

Walsh, Fergus. Vegetative Patient Scott Routley Says, "I'm not in Pain." *BBC News*, November 12, 2012. www.bbc.uk/news/health-20268044?print=true.

Weiskrantz, Lawrence, and Davies, Martin, eds. *Frontiers of Consciousness*. Oxford: Oxford University Press, 2008.

Wiffen, Philip, Derry, Sheena, and Moore, R. Andrew. Impact of Morphine, Fentanyl, Oxycodone or Codeine on Patient Consciousness, Appetite and Thirst When Used to Treat Cancer Pain. *Cochrane Database of Systematic Reviews* 5 (2014): CD011056. Cited by Takla, Savulescu, and Wilkinson, 2021, p. 285, n. 12.

Wilkinson, Dominic. Dissonance and Consonance about Death. *Journal of Medical Ethics* 47 (2021): 231–2.

Wilkinson, Dominic, and Savulescu, Julian. Should We Allow Organ Donation Euthanasia? Alternatives for Maximizing the Number and Quality of Organs for Transplantation. *Bioethics* 26 (2012): 32–48.

Wilkinson, Dominic, and Savulescu, Julian. Is it Better to be Minimally Conscious than Vegetative? *Journal of Medical Ethics* 39 (2013): 557–8.

*Winkfield* v. *Children's Hospital Oakland*. Case No. C13-5993, US District Court, Northern District of California, Oakland, filed December 30, 2013.

Wittgenstein, Ludwig. *Tractatus Logico-Philosophicus*, trans. D. F. Pears and B. F. McGuinness. London: Routledge, 1921/1974.

Wittmann, Marc. The Inner Sense of Time: How the Brain Creates a Representation of Duration. *Nature Reviews Neuroscience* 14 (2013): 217–23.

Wittmann, Marc. *Felt Time: The Science of How We Experience Time*, trans. E. Butler. Cambridge, MA: MIT Press, 2016.

Wittmann, Marc. *Altered States of Consciousness: Experiences Out of Time and Self*, trans. P. Hurd. Cambridge, MA: MIT Press, 2018.

Woodward, Paul, ed. *The Doctrine of Double Effect: Philosophers Debate a Controversial Moral Principle*. Notre Dame: Notre Dame University Press, 2001.

Young, Michael, Bodien, Yelena, Giacino, Joseph et al. The Neuroethics of Disorders of Consciousness: A Brief History of Evolving Ideas. *Brain* 144 (2021): 3291–3310.

Young, Michael, Bodien, Yelena, and Edlow, Brian. Ethical Considerations in Clinical Trials for Disorders of Consciousness. *Brain Sciences* 12 (2022): 211. http: doi.org/10.3390/brainsci12020211.

Zadra, Antonio, Desautels, Alex, Petit, Dominique, and Montplaisir, Jacques. Somnambulism: Clinical Aspects and Pathophysiological Hypotheses. *The Lancet Neurology* 12 (2013): 285–94.

Zeman, Adam. Does Consciousness Spring from the Brain? Dilemmas of Awareness in Practice and in Theory. In Weiskrantz and Davies (eds.), 2008, pp. 289–322.

# Acknowledgments

I thank Thomasine Kushner for inviting me to write this Element and her encouragement and continued support, and Julia Ford, my Content Manager at Cambridge University Press. James Bernat and Georg Northoff, provided very helpful comments on the manuscript. I am grateful to them for their thoughtful and constructive reviews. I thank Alexandra Sellers for discussion of ethical issues in restoring consciousness near the end of life and Teresa Yu for discussion of all aspects of consciousness. Sections of "The Moral Insignificance of Death in Organ Donation," *Cambridge Quarterly of Healthcare Ethics*, Volume 22, 2013, Number 2, pp. 192–202, "The Value and Disvalue of Consciousness," *Cambridge Quarterly of Healthcare Ethics*, Volume 25, 2016, Number 4, pp. 600–612, and *The Neuroethics of Memory: From Total Recall to Oblivion,* Cambridge University Press, 2019, 234p. have been reproduced in this work with permission from Cambridge University Press.

Cambridge Elements ≡

# Bioethics and Neuroethics

### Thomasine Kushner

*California Pacific Medical Center, San Francisco*

Thomasine Kushner, PhD, is the founding Editor of the *Cambridge Quarterly of Healthcare Ethics* and coordinates the International Bioethics Retreat, where bioethicists share their current research projects, the Cambridge Consortium for Bioethics Education, a growing network of global bioethics educators, and the Cambridge-ICM Neuroethics Network, which provides a setting for leading brain scientists and ethicists to learn from each other.

### About the Series

Bioethics and neuroethics play pivotal roles in today's debates in philosophy, science, law, and health policy. With the rapid growth of scientific and technological advances, their importance will only increase. This series provides focused and comprehensive coverage in both disciplines consisting of foundational topics, current subjects under discussion and views toward future developments.

# Cambridge Elements ≡

## Bioethics and Neuroethics

Printed in the United States
by Baker & Taylor Publisher Services